# EMERGENCY RESPONSE TO CRISIS

**Executive Editor:** Jim Yvorra
**Production Editor:** Michael J. Rogers
**Art and Cover Design:** Don Sellers, AMI

# EMERGENCY RESPONSE TO CRISIS

## A crisis intervention guidebook for emergency service personnel

Jeffrey T. Mitchell, Ph.D.

*and*

H. L. P. Resnik, M.D., F.A.C.P., F.A.P.A.

Emergency Response to Crisis

 **CHEVRON PUBLISHING CORPORATION**
**5018 Dorsey Hall Drive, Suite 104**
**Ellicott City, MD 21042**

Library of Congress Cataloging in Publication Data

Mitchell, Jeffrey T.
     Emergency response to crisis.
     Includes index.
     1. Crisis intervention. (Psychiatry)  2. Police, social
work.
L. Resnik, H.L.P., joint author.  II. Title.
RC480.5.M57   362.2'04256   80-20079
ISBN 1-883581-11-7

Prentice-Hall International, Inc., London
Prentice-Hall of Australia, Pty., Ltd., Sydney
Prentice-Hall of India Private Limited, New Delhi
Prentice-Hall of Japan, Inc., Tokyo
Prentice-Hall of Southeast Asia Pte. Ltd., Singapore
Whitehall Books, Limited, Petone, New Zealand

Printed in the United States of America
00  15 14 13 12 11 10

To the Mitchell family, especially my parents Rita and Loren; and to Pete and Mary Jo, good friends

JTM

To the memory of Celia Greenberg Resnik and her grandchildren
Rebecca, Seth, and Jessica

HLPR

# CONTENTS

# FOREWORD

The publication of *Emergency Response to Crisis* is a most welcome tool in the field of Emergency Medical Services. Such a book is long overdue. This compact text offers Emergency Service personnel a ready reference for assessing and dealing with the emotional responses inherent in any human crisis situation.

Emergency Service personnel have a difficult and often thankless task in providing services to those who call for help. In addition to the many important issues presented here, this unique text addresses the issue of job stress. It considers the emotional impact that continued exposure to human crisis has on the crisis worker. The final chapter is devoted to self-assessment and offers some self-sustaining, coping mechanisms one can utilize in attempting to reduce the negative effects of work related stress.

This book is a landmark in the field and the authors and editor are to be congratulated for their concise, practical, and theoretically sound presentations.

R Adams Cowley, M.D.
Director
Maryland Institute for Emergency Medical Services Systems
Baltimore, Maryland

# PREFACE

In July of 1972, Harvey L. P. Resnik M.D., was appointed chief of the new Mental Health Emergencies Section, the successor program to the Center for Studies of Suicide Prevention, within the National Institute of Mental Health (NIMH). The new section rapidly became aware that there was very little mental health emergency preparation in the training of emergency and rescue personnel.

One year later, the Emergency Medical Services (EMS) program of the Department of Health, Education, and Welfare began its operations. This agency also recognized the serious need for mental health emergency training and sought out and continued opportunities to satisfy this need within the limitations of EMS systems.

In January 1973, an NIMH Ad Hoc Committee compiled a textbook, *Emergency Psychiatric Care*, a training and reference manual to correct that deficiency. However, feedback from field workers indicated that the book did not satisfy their need for practical, specific, and easily retainable techniques in a book form that was suitable for carrying and fitting into a kit or glove compartment.

In 1975, Jeff Mitchell, as a Maryland Regional EMS Coordinator, invited Dr. Resnik to conduct portions of a training seminar for EMT instructors on mental health emergencies. The following year, at Dr. Resnik's invitation, Jeff Mitchell taught segments in behavioral emergencies workshops for emergency personnel in Virginia, Maryland, and the District of Columbia. During these workshops and with the Brady Company's support, Dr. Resnik was encouraged to produce a more practical mental health emergency handbook. He enlisted Jeff Mitchell, a certified EMT instructor with a Master's degree in psychology, as co-author because of his very strong understanding of, and familiarity with, the field requirements. As the project developed, Jeff Mitchell's time commitment to it made it obvious that he should be recognized as senior author/editor.

This book is the product of three years of research and writing in the field of crisis intervention. It offers the most current information on assessment and management of various crises commonly encountered by emergency service personnel. The book, in many respects, may actually be considered a comprehensive course, and the authors hope it will be utilized as a classroom text, as well as a guidebook by field personnel. The material in this book has already been used to train over five hundred emergency service personnel in Virginia, Maryland, Pennsylvania, and the District of Columbia.

The authors welcome the advice and comments from those who use the book. Without doubt, subsequent editions will need to be changed to better accommodate the needs of field personnel.

The Authors

# ACKNOWLEDGEMENTS

Grateful acknowledgement is made to all who have given so freely of their time and energy to assure the success of this work. It is impossible to individually acknowledge all who have helped with every aspect of the book, but some people deserve a special word of thanks for their role in the preparation of the manuscript. It is with heartfelt gratitude that the contributions of the following people are recognized.

Sincere thanks go to Mary Claire Brown for her assistance in organizing and analyzing the survey which was sent to emergency service personnel in the early stages of the project. Special thanks also go to the technical advisors, Louis Jordan, Ronald Schaffer, Dr. Denis Madden and Attorney Robert Carr for their generous advice and practical guidelines.

A world of gratitude is owed to Carol Ann Sybert who spent uncountable hours typing and patiently retyping the majority of the manuscript and who provided vital assistance in the manuscript graphics. Thanks also to Cindy Gibson and June Mitchell, who typed portions of the manuscript.

The volunteer work of Lorraine Cheban, Peter Giulioni and his lovely wife, Mary Jo, was an enormous contribution. They worked many hours to carefully proofread and edit the manuscript. Their work will not be forgotten and will always be appreciated.

A special note of thanks to Carolyn Marie Harding who not only prepared the index of the book and proofread portions of the manuscript, but who also offered emotional support and encouragement during particularly critical periods in the writing of the book. Without her understanding the last chapters would have been considerably more difficult to write.

Finally, Lawrence Messier deserves special recognition for agreeing to join the project late in its development. His professional writing and his enthusiasm for the work prevented excessive delays in the overall project.

The contributions of these friends and others, who have not been mentioned here, but whose work is deeply appreciated, are priceless. They cannot be adequately repaid. They can only be cherished for a lifetime!

My deepest appreciation,

Jeff

# ACKNOWLEDGEMENT

I would like to acknowledge the very special efforts made by Clark J. Hudak, M.S.W., for his professional input into the content of this book. I appreciate very much the consultations provided by Diane Daskel Ruben, J.D., on the legal aspects of medical emergency care. A special thanks is due Sarah Bitzer, our office manager, who coordinated the efforts in processing the questionnaire throughout the country, as well as our typist support. My thanks to the office staff who pitched in so selflessly: Evelyn Noble Hudson, Ruth Gross, Marion Taylor, Gail Moore, Debbie Holt, Paula Perry, Jane Latter, and Karen Schlegel, R.N.

I do not believe a more committed veteran team can be found anywhere that is more adept in converting concepts and ideas written from various sized papers in classically undecipherable medical prescription hand writing than this team. I am most grateful to them.

H. L. P. Resnik, M.D.

# INTRODUCTION

One of the most frequently neglected areas in the training of emergency service personnel is that of crisis intervention. This viewpoint was expressed in 1975 by Dr. Calvin Frederick, Director of the Mental Health Disaster Section of the National Institute of Mental Health. He wrote an article entitled, "System Response to Behavioral Emergencies" in which he stated that the personnel, ". . . who provide ambulance, fire, or police service, are almost totally unprepared to render psychological first aid in the management of acute mental problems. There is an absence of training in psychological disturbances, not only among ambulance, fire, and law enforcement personnel, but also among emergency room personnel . . ."

This view was strongly supported by the results of a survey which was mailed by the authors of this book to 250 emergency service personnel across the nation. Eighty career and volunteer personnel responded to the survey. To the first question on the survey, "What is your greatest problem when you are required to work with an emotionally stressful situation?", sixty-four (80 percent of the respondents) answered "a lack of training."

Other serious problems listed by respondents in the survey included the absence of clear cut guidelines for the field management and transportation of the victims of emotional crisis and the lack of twenty-four hour professional resources for field consultation. Public safety personnel also reported that they frequently experience difficulties with the assessment of crisis victims. They lack self confidence and are distressed by their own personal anxiety, which is produced by a limited knowledge of basic human communication skills and an inadequate understanding of a variety of crisis situations.

*Emergency Response to Crisis* has two specific aims. First, it will provide not only the necessary theoretical background for understanding crisis, but will also show the practical guidelines for the proper management of a variety of crisis events. Secondly, it aims at assisting crisis workers in recognizing, understanding, and coping with their own emotional reactions to the job related and personal crises which they are called upon to manage.

It is impossible for a book of this nature to provide specific information for each case encountered in the field. Human beings are complex, and each incident is going to be unique. There are, however, significant similarities in humans who are faced with stressful situations, and those similarities form the basis from which many of the guidelines in this book have been drawn. Not all of the guidelines presented in this book will have equal application in every state and every jurisdiction. Local policies, laws, regulations, and operating procedures should be followed whenever the guidelines in the book are in conflict with those policies and procedures.

The book is divided into fifteen specific topical chapters such as suicide, sexual assault, child abuse, and alcohol and substance abuse. Each chapter provides background information essential in developing an adequate understanding of that particular crisis problem. In addition, each chapter contains suggested methods for the assessment and care of a crisis victim. A "Rapid Reference" section can be found in the back of the book. This special section has been designed to provide a quick overlook of the specific crisis problems discussed in the book. It provides a list of the most important intervention guidelines.

The application of guidelines provided in this book will enable emergency service personnel to manage a host of crisis incidents in a safe and efficient manner. The victims of crisis who are cared for according to these guidelines will benefit most in that they will generally be faced with substantially less long-term emotional disabilities and will emerge from the crisis as stronger, healthier people.

# ABOUT THE AUTHORS

*Jeffrey T. Mitchell, Ph.D.*
Dr. Mitchell is an assistant professor of Emergency Health Services at the University of Maryland Baltimore County. He is a consultant psychologist to the Maryland Institute for Emergency Medical Services Systems. He also serves as a fire service psychologist for the Howard County (Maryland) Fire Department. He is a certified Emergency Medical Technician Instructor and a former fire fighter/paramedic. Dr. Mitchell is an adjunct faculty member of the National Emergency Training Center of the Federal Emergency Management Agency and has lectured throughout the United States and in several foreign countries. He developed the Critical Incident Stress Debriefing process for emergency personnel and has numerous publications in the emergency field. Dr. Mitchell holds a master degree in counseling psychology, an advanced graduate certificate in clinical psychology and a Ph.D. in human development.

*H. L. P. Resnik, M.D., F.A.C.P., F.A.P.A.*
Dr. Resnik is the clinical director and administrator of Associated Mental Consultants, Ltd., a private practice group in College Park, Maryland. He formerly served as Chief, Center for Studies of Suicide Prevention and Mental Health Emergencies, National Institute of Mental Health. He is also Clinical Professor of Psychiatry, School of Medicine, George Washington University and Lecturer in Psychiatry at the School of Medicine, Johns Hopkins University. He is a psychiatric consultant to the Maryland Institute for Emergency Medical Services, and the Council of Governments, Department of Defense, and Naval Medical Center, District of Columbia. Dr. Resnik is a fellow of the American College of Psychiatrists and the American Psychiatric Association. He has edited *Emergency Psychiatric Care: The Management of Mental Health Crisis, The Prediction of Suicide,* and *Suicidal Behaviors: Diagnosis and Management.* Dr. Resnik has edited seven books and over 60 chapters and articles in the mental health field.

# CONTRIBUTORS

*Margaret M. Epperson-Sebour, M.S.W., A.C.S.W.*
Chief, Family Services, Maryland Institute for Emergency Medical Services, Baltimore, Maryland.

*Clark J. Hudak, M.S.W.*
Therapist, Associated Mental Health Consultants, Ltd., College Park, Maryland.

*Denis J. Madden, Ph.D.*
Director, Clinical Research Program for Violent Behavior, Institute of Psychiatry and Human Behavior, University of Maryland School of Medicine, Baltimore, Maryland.

*Lawrence D. Messier, M.A.*
Counseling Staff, Catonsville, Community College, Catonsville, Maryland. Ph.D. candidate, Human Development Program, University of Maryland.

*Jeffrey T. Mitchell, Ph.D.*
Assistant Professor, Emergency Health Services Department, University of Maryland Baltimore County. Consultant Psychologist, Maryland Insitute for Emergency Medical Services Systems, Baltimore Maryland. Fire Psychologist, Howard County Fire Department, Maryland.

*Ann Scanlon-Schilpp, R.N., M.S.*
Clinical Specialist in Psychiatric Nursing, Maryland Institute for Emergency Medical Services, Baltimore, Maryland.

# CLARIFICATION OF TERMINOLOGY

The English language does not provide a generic singular pronoun meaning "he" or "she" which is equivalent to the plural "they". Therefore, "he" and "she" will be used in the generic sense and should be understood to imply both sexes. The use of the generic "he" or "she" will avoid awkward sentence structure. Except where the context obviously implies a specific gender, all words importing one gender intend the other as well.

# CHAPTER 1

# *Understanding Crisis*

Jeffrey T. Mitchell, M.S.

## THE NORMAL RANGE OF BEHAVIOR

Although this book contains a chapter dealing with severely mentally disturbed people (psychotics and neurotics), it was not written exclusively as a management guide for these cases. For the most part, the book was written to assist emergency service personnel in dealing with average people, within the "normal" range of behavior, who are suddenly thrown into a crisis as a result of a high level of stress in their lives.

It has been noted by a number of authors that practically every emergency call has emotional aspects to it. Therefore, some basic understanding of the common human response to emotional crises is essential for every public safety worker. Figure 1.1 indicates that approximately three-quarters of the calls answered by public safety personnel are for the care of average people, not psychotics (severely mentally disturbed people). In fact, only a very small number of calls are made for the management of psychotics. This is because, in actuality, psychotics make up a small segment of the total population. The total number of psychotics in the United States is estimated to be just over a million and more than half of these are in institutions or special community based programs. [1-4]

A larger, but less serious, group of emotionally disturbed individuals is the neurotics (moderately emotionally disturbed people who are having problems in one or more areas of their lives, but who are not so disturbed as to need institutionalization). There are approximately ten million neurotics in the United States. [4] Together, these two groups make up less than ten percent of the entire population.

At the other end of the spectrum of human behavior are approximately ten million people who are above average or extraordinary (gifted) in their behavior. (This discussion is not about in-

1

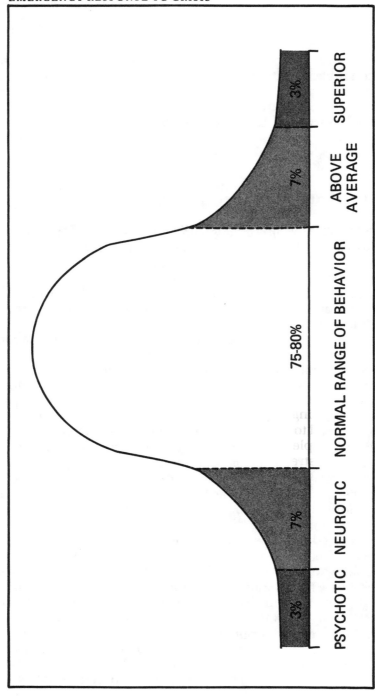

*Figure 1.1.   Continuum of human behavior measured in percentage of population*

telligence levels. It simply refers to behavior. It is possible to have a very intelligent psychotic!)

Approximately eighty percent of the population are people who function quite well on a day to day basis. They are the average people who think, work, play, have families, and live in society. This large segment of the population is the group that will be served most by public safety personnel during crisis situations. Any unnecessary concerns about dealing with a great number of psychotics should be laid to rest.

## THE STEADY STATE

Most people live their everyday lives in a balanced or steady state. They have some degree of harmony in their thoughts, feelings, wishes, and physical needs. This steady state is sometimes called equilibrium. This state will continue as long as there is no major interruption or interference from outside factors. Even after interruption, a person or group tends to return to the original state of equilibrium as quickly as possible.

The steady state is usually characterized by a balance between the two mental systems of emotions and thoughts. The two systems are never perfectly balanced but there is considerable harmony between them (see Figure 1.2).

Under stress, the harmony of the steady state breaks down and the feelings get out of control. The thought system fails and people tend to regress or go backwards in their level of behavior. That is, people who are average tend to act more neurotic when faced with stress. They are generally less logical and find it difficult to reason their way out of trouble. They may even become temporarily psychotic. [5-7]

## WHAT IS A CRISIS?

Any serious interruption in the steady state or equilibrium of a person, family, or group is considered a crisis. *A crisis is a state of emotional turmoil*. It is also considered an emotionally significant event which acts as a turning point for better or worse in a person's life.

Anyone can experience a crisis at anytime in his life. A crisis is always real to the person who is experiencing it even though it may not appear so to the people around him. There are two

3

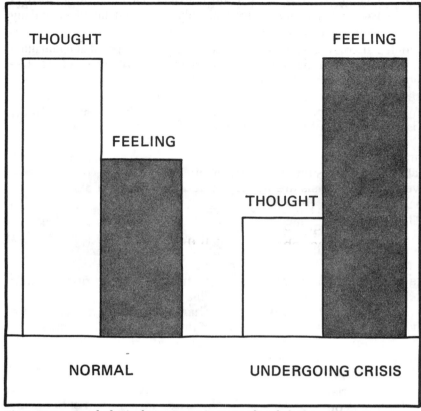

*Figure 1-2.  Psychological processes in normal and abnormal situations.*

major types of crises. The first is called "maturational" and includes experiences like puberty, adolescence, marriage, and growing old. The second type of crisis is called "sudden disruptive", or "situational," and includes divorce, death, accident, and illness. [7-9]

## CHARACTERISTICS OF ALL CRISES

Emotional crises have four main characteristics.

1. They are sudden.
2. The individual, family, or group is not adequately prepared to handle the event and the normal methods of dealing (coping) with stress fail.

4

3. Crises are short in duration. Most crises last only twenty-four to thirty-six hours and only in rare situations are they longer than six weeks.

4. Emotional crises have the potential to produce dangerous, self-destructive, or socially unacceptable behavior. [7,10]

## STAGES OF CRISES

Almost all crises occur with some similarities. Many researchers have discussed specific stages or phases of crisis. The following five phases of crisis are usually noted (see Figure 1.3).

1. The *precrisis* phase in which the person is in a general state of equilibrium.

2. The *impact* phase in which the stressful event occurred.

3. The *crisis phase.* The person in this phase is aware of the stressful event and perceives it as a threat. This phase has two parts:
   A. Confusion and disorganization.
   B. Trial and error reorganization.

4. The *resolution* phase in which the person regains control over his emotions and works toward a solution.

5. The *post crisis* phase in which the person comes out of the crisis and resumes normal activities. Some people remain permanently emotionally injured by the crisis experience, (B) while others are made stronger and healthier (A). [7,10–12]

## THE VICTIM'S RESPONSE TO CRISIS

Emergency service personnel need a working knowledge of the effects of severe stress and crisis on the average person. Without this knowledge they are prone to underestimate their critical role in managing crises. The assistance provided by emergency service personnel has deep and lasting effects upon the victims.

Victims of crisis are vulnerable to permanent damage as a result of continued stress. They are also receptive to assistance during the crisis. Assistance provided by public safety personnel during the first one to three hours of the crisis is often more sig-

5

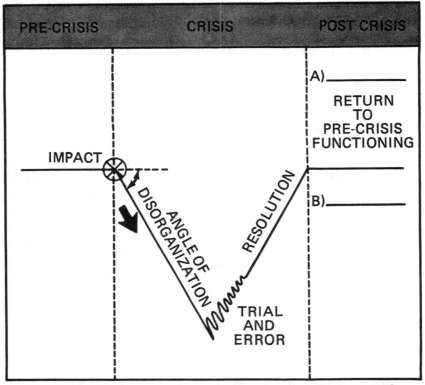

*Figure 1.3.    Stages of crisis. (from Resnik HLP, Ruben HL: Emergency Psychiatric Care. Bowie, MD; The Charles Press, Inc., 1975)*

nificant in terms of the overall crisis than much of the help which is provided later by hospital staff and counselors. [10]

Most people who undergo crises experience the following six phases of emotional reaction (see Figure 1.4):

1. High anxiety or emotional shock
2. Denial
3. Anger
4. Remorse
5. Grief
6. Reconciliation [13]

It should be noted that the order provided here is the typical order. Sometimes these emotional reactions are mixed together and sometimes they are repeated.

Crisis workers usually encounter victims in the field during the first three phases of the crisis reaction. They see the victims when they are experiencing high anxiety, denial, and anger (the three phases when the victims are most receptive to assistance).

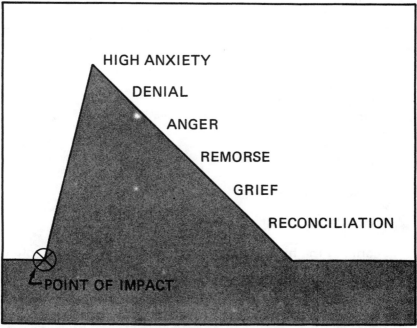

*Figure 1.4.    Emotional response to crisis. (from Epperson MM: Families in sudden crisis. Social Work in Health Care, Vols. 2 and 3, Spring 1977)*

## ASSESSMENT AND GENERAL INTERVENTION TECHNIQUES

*High Anxiety Or Emotional Shock.* Victims in this phase of the crisis reaction fall into two main groups. They are either hysterical and very active or they are stunned, inactive, and depressed.

Common signs and symptoms of those in the active group are:

- Agitation
- Wringing of the hands
- Loud screaming or crying
- Hyperactivity
- Nausea
- Vomiting

- Rapid speech
- Rapid breathing
- Flushed face
- Emotionally out of control. [14]

The inactive crisis victim usually exhibits these signs and symptoms (similar to the signs of shock):

- Inactivity
- Fainting
- Nausea/vomiting
- Staring into space
- Dull eyes
- Low blood pressure
- Rapid, thready pulse
- Sweating
- Cold clammy skin
- Pale appearance
- Wandering about aimlessly.

People in the high anxiety-emotional shock stage are often likely to return to burning buildings for trivial items, frequently interfere with police and fire-rescue operations and may be combative. Each person may have a unique response to a crisis, but most exhibit the signs and symptoms described above. [2,13,15]

Crisis victims experiencing the high anxiety-emotional shock phase are best managed in the following ways:

- Remove the victim from the scene to a less threatening, more secure environment.
- Reassure the victim that you are there to help.
- Talk to the victim.
- Touch them if appropriate.
- Direct them to do specific, task oriented actions. For example, tell them to "move", "sit down", "lie down", "hold this", and answer your questions.

Other intervention techniques will be discussed at a greater length in the chapters dealing with specific problems.

*Denial Phase.* Denial is a normal response to stressful situations. It is a protective mechanism which prevents too much from happening too fast. Even very sick or seriously injured people tend to do this. A good example is the heart attack victim who attributes his pains to indigestion. Another example of denial is the parents of a young drug abuser who tell the police that their son could not be involved in a crime because he is "such a good boy." [13,16]

The denying victim of crisis is best managed by the following:

- Allow the person to deny, but do not agree with him.
- Gently and carefully tell the facts.
- Be prepared to repeat again and again.
- Do not promise things that may not happen. For example, do not say "Everything will be all right." It may not!
- Be compassionate and understanding.

*Anger Phase.* Anger is the normal human response to frustration. When people feel that they cannot cope with a situation, they usually feel overwhelmed and frustrated. Frustration quickly turns into anger. If the anger is not expressed properly, it may eventually turn into aggression. [4]

People may first direct their anger at others and things that are not close to them because it is easier than turning the anger towards a person they love or themselves. They may, for instance, be angry at the rainstorm which they feel caused the accident. It is easier than being angry at their eighteen-year-old son who was using the car without their permission.

Unfortunately, people are not always careful to direct their anger where it belongs. They frequently focus it on the emergency service personnel who are most concerned with helping them. This is a normal reaction because the people feeling angry are overwhelmed by the crisis, are not thinking clearly, and do not know how to express their anger in a more appropriate manner. [13]

In handling the angry crisis victim the following guidelines should be kept in mind:

- Do not take their anger personally. It is really not directed at you.
- Let them express themselves verbally.
- Do not let a victim of crisis strike you (it makes them feel very guilty later).
- Show confidence. Tell them that you understand that they are angry and frustrated, but that you are there now and that you will do your best to help them.

9

- Do not argue with the crisis victim. You cannot win against an emotion.

*Remorse, Grief, and Reconciliation Phases.* It is not likely that crisis workers will find people in the last three phases of crisis—remorse, grief, and reconciliation. It usually takes longer for these phases to develop. Victims are then being treated by medical, legal, or social service staffs when they do occur. For the sake of continuity, however, these three phases will be briefly discussed here.

The remorse phase is one that has elements of guilt and sorrow. It is easily recognized by the "if only" statements which victims of crisis tend to make. They frequently say, "If only I had not done this or that." [13]
Remorse is best handled by:

- Careful listening
- Reassurance
- Avoiding judgmental statements
- Allowing the person to express himself.

Grief is the first real stage of healing. People need to grieve losses before they can move on with their lives. It is a necessary step and it helps the person to recover.
If a victim happens to be in deep grief when the crisis worker arrives, it is best to handle it by:

- Allowing the person to express his or her feelings.
- Providing a good listening ear.
- Assuring the person that it is OK to feel bad.
- Avoiding sedation unless it is absolutely necessary and only when ordered by a doctor.
- Being caring and supportive.

If the crisis worker has been helpful in allowing the victim of crisis to grieve, it is likely that the person will pass through the grief process and reach the phase of reconciliation quicker. Reconciliation occurs when the crisis is resolved and the person returns to at least the same level at which he functioned before the crisis. If enough help was given, he may be a better person. If not, he may never regain his original state of equilibrium. [13]

10

## CRISIS INTERVENTION

The helping response of a crisis worker to a victim of crisis is called *crisis intervention.* Crisis intervention is an active but temporary entry into the life situation of an individual, a family, or a group during a period of stress. [17]

There are two important elements of this definition. First, crisis intervention is *active.* Emergency service personnel have to be alert, flexible, resourceful, and willing to get involved in an active role. They may have to take a portion of control over another's life for a short time during a stressful period. Secondly, crisis intervention is *temporary.* Crises are time limited. In most cases, a rescuer will only have an hour or less to work on a case. This limits the efforts to the immediate problem and to the directly related behaviors. [10,12]

## GOALS OF CRISIS INTERVENTION

Rescuers have three objectives in dealing with practically any crisis. They are:

    A. Shield the crisis victim from any additional stress.

    B. Assist the victim in organizing and mobilizing his resources (family and community).

    C. Return the victim, as much as possible, to a pre-crisis level of functioning. [9,10,12]

## CRISIS INTERVENTION BLUE PRINT

Crisis intervention is not a sloppy, haphazard approach to helping people. In spite of its flexibility and the difficulty of dealing with such an enormous number of personalities, crisis intervention follows a structure which contains five major components:

    A. Assessment

    B. Plan

    C. Implementation

    D. Reassessment

    E. Recapping [12,18]

11

## Assessment

This is a very brief sizing up of the problem. What has happened? Who is involved? What was the cause? How serious is the problem? All these questions need to be answered quickly.

## High Priority Factors

- Is there clear and imminent danger to the crisis worker?
- Is victim's life or limb(s) in danger?
- Are others, either involved in or near the scene, in danger? Are there complicating dangers such as fire, environmental factors, traffic, crowds, or other factors? [2,15,19]

## Secondary Factors

- What is the current problem?
- How many people are involved?
- Who are the main characters?
- Who are the witnesses?
- Is this a criminal situation?
  A. Can the victim provide a brief description of the suspect?
  B. Does he know the direction of escape?
  C. How long ago did the incident take place?
- Any other factors which should be considered? [2,15,19,20]

More detailed expositions of assessment techniques will be provided in the chapters which follow, especially in the chapters dealing with communication skills and history taking.

## The Plan

The next step in managing a crisis is to make a preliminary plan of action based on the assessment of the situation. Even if the assessment is incomplete, it is necessary to do something. As noted earlier, crisis victims are open to assistance. Almost any plan which is prudent and reasonable will tend to be helpful in a crisis. No crisis plan needs to be detailed. The crisis will not wait. Doing something positive is more helpful than doing nothing where crises are concerned.

## Implementation of the Plan

*Act! Intervene!* The key to successful crisis management is *action.* Whatever the plan, get it going. Delay is dangerous for the crisis victim, so do something, do not just stand there. [10,20]

## Reassessment

Once a plan has been implemented, it needs to be checked out to see if it is working. If it is working, it should be kept going. If it is failing to work, it may be producing harm, and it should be abandoned. The situation should be evaluated again for new information. A new plan should be formulated quickly and implemented as soon as possible if the initial plan is not working.

## Recapping

Victims of crisis have an extremely difficult time following all of the action going on around them. They usually need someone to tell them what has happened, what is being done about it, and what is probably going to happen next. Frequently, recapping must be done over and over again. [18]

### REFERENCES

1. Frederick CJ: Crisis intervention and emergency mental health. *In* Johnson WR (ed): Health In Action. New York; Holt, Rinehart, and Winston, 1977
2. The Committee on Allied Health, American Academy of Orthopaedic Surgeons: The disturbed and unruly patient. *In* Emergency Care and Transportation of the Sick and Injured, 2nd ed.

Menasha, WI; George Banta Co., 1977
3. Bard M, Illisan K: Crisis intervention and investigation of forcible rape. *In* Police Chief, Vol. XLI No. 5, May 1974
4. Coleman JC: Major maladjustive patterns. *In* Psychology and Effective Behavior. Glenview, IL; Scott, Foresman, and Company, 1969
5. Parad HJ (ed): Crisis Intervention: Selected Readings. New York, Family Service Association of America, 1976
6. Bowen M: Family Therapy in Clinical Practice. New York, Jason Aronson, Inc., 1978
7. Rappaport L: The state of crisis: Some theoretical consideration. *In* The Social Service Review, Vol. XXXV No. 2, 1962
8. Ruben HL: C.I.: Crisis Intervention. New York, Popular Library, 1976
9. Caplan G, Codder V: The turning points of life. McCall's, October 1966
10. Cain A: Crisis theory and intervention. Mississippi Nurse, November 1973
11. Hill R: Generic features of families under stress. Social Casework, Vol. XXXIX Nos. 2 and 3, 1958
12. Resnik HLP, Ruben H (eds): Emergency Psychiatric Care, The Management of Mental Health Crises. Bowie, MD; The Charles Press Publishers, Inc., 1975
13. Epperson MM: Families in sudden crisis. Social Work in Health Care, Vols. 2 and 3, Spring 1977
14. Holsti OR: Crisis, stress and decision-making. International Social Science Journal, Vol. 23, 1971
15. Grant H, Murray R: Emergency Care, 2nd ed., Bowie, MD; Robert J. Brady Co., 1978
16. Coleman JC: Reactions to adjustment demands. *In* Psychology and Effective Behavior. Glenview, IL; Scott, Foresman, and Company, 1969
17. Parad HJ: Introduction to Crisis Intervention. *In* Parad HJ (ed): Crisis Intervention: Selected Readings. New York, Family Service Association of America, 1965
18. Parad HJ: Preventive casework: Problems and Implications. *In* Parad HJ (ed): Crisis Intervention: Selected Readings. New York, Family Services Association of America, 1965
19. Gazzaniga AB, Iseri LT, Baren M: Emergency Care: Principles and Practices for the EMT-Paramedic. Reston, VA; Reston Publishing Co., Inc., 1979
20. Bard M: The Function of the Police in Crisis Intervention and Conflict Management. Washington, DC; US Department of Justice, National Institute of Law Enforcement and Criminal Justice, 1975

# CHAPTER **2**

# *Human Communications Skills, Interviewing Techniques, and Assessment*

Jeffrey T. Mitchell, M.S.

## INTRODUCTION

The ability to communicate carefully is, by far, the most essential element of all crisis intervention. The proper field management of all situations calls for the ability of crisis workers to assess the situation, devise a plan of action, and enlist the cooperation of the victim. They must be able to provide emotional support while listening carefully to the victim's emotional and physical needs.

The task of careful communication is complicated by a number of factors. Frequently, training in effective communications has been limited or nonexistent. The variability of each situation demands great flexibility on the part of crisis workers. Most importantly, the emotions generated within the crisis worker by the victim or the situation may interfere with his efforts to intervene in the crisis.

This chapter has been written in an attempt to organize the essential elements of communication skills, and interviewing techniques, in such a manner that emergency service personnel might have at their disposal a set of guidelines for intervention in almost any crisis. These guidelines are the basic tools of victim assessment. Used properly, they will help to boost crisis worker confidence and will reduce the risks of mismanaging emotional crises.

## I. HUMAN COMMUNICATION SKILLS

### A. Background

Human communications can be a very complex process. There are three essential elements in human communications:

A sender → A message → A receiver

The sender transmits a specific message which may come in a verbal, nonverbal, or behavior form. Sending the message is only one part of the process. The sender intends to get a response from the receiver. The communication is effective if the message has been received as it was originally intended. [1]

This may sound somewhat simple, but it is considerably more complex. Even in calm, secure situations, communications with people we know can get confused. There are barriers to good communications. Some common blockades to communication are the issues of:

- Personal goals
- Personal identification
- Power
- Rapport

Others are:

- Attitudes
- Prejudices
- Frame of reference
- Language skills
- Comfort of the speaker and listener. [1]

These blockades affect not only the sender, but also the receiver. Some of the less obvious communication blockades will be more fully explained in the following sections, as will the methods of improving communications.

## B. Communication Blockades

*Personal goals.* Each person involved in any communication has some personal goals. They may be for the fulfillment of physical needs such as food and clothing, or for the assurances of security. Other goals are for social contact or for self-fulfillment. The more closely balanced the goals of the crisis victim and the ability of the crisis worker to fulfill them, the better the communication.

*Personal Identification.* If the rescue worker sees himself as a member of a helping team, he has a good chance of assisting the victim. His chances decline if he feels isolated and not part of the team. The victim also has difficulty in cooperating if he feels isolated and uncared for by the rescuers.

16

*Power.* Who is in control? If a victim feels out of control and does not perceive that the crisis worker is exerting some control, communications will fail.

*Rapport.* Sometimes a crisis worker has to communicate a bit of himself with the victim to get effective communications in motion. He needs to make a good introduction and to show some genuine concern. Establishing rapport for a good working relationship is essential. [1-6]

*Attitudes, Prejudices, and the Frame of Reference.* These are the most serious blockades to good communications. They are each individual's way of looking at situations. They are based on a person's education, family life, training, friends, environment, culture, code of ethics, and all of his experiences both painful and pleasant. [3] These things make a person unique. There is no "good" or "bad" frame of reference. They just exist, and form the basis on which a person functions in his thoughts, feelings, and actions.

The frames of reference of crisis workers often keep the crisis worker from hearing what a victim has to say. They are things that make the crisis workers think that this or that particular situation is not really a crisis, while the victim thinks it is the worst thing that has ever happened.

Communication becomes successful when the crisis worker can partially and temporarily suspend his own frame of reference and hear the needs, fears, hopes, and pain of the crisis victim.

*Language Skills.* If the speaker is using language too difficult to understand, communication is not going to be effective.

*Comfort of Speaker and Listener.* If the crisis worker or the victim have too much anxiety, or if they are physically uncomfortable, communication is limited.

*Environmental Distractions.* An inattentive crisis worker will not achieve the goals of the communication.

## C. Goals of Crisis Communications

1. Get the victim to talk freely and frankly.
2. Help the victim to talk about what is important in the

17

*present situation.*

3. Obtain as much background information concerning the problem as possible.
4. Help the victim to understand the situation in which he is involved.
5. Assist the victim in finding alternatives that will help to resolve the problem.

## D. Listening Techniques

The techniques listed here will assist the crisis worker in improving his communication skills. Examples have been provided wherever they might improve the crisis worker's understanding of the techniques.

1. *Desire to Listen.* If a person does not want to listen, he will not (even if the other person is yelling).
2. *Prepare to Listen.* Choose a quiet place. Get the crowd to move back. Cut down distractions and interruptions.
3. *Show interest.* Here are some examples:

   - "Can you tell me what is upsetting you? I'd like to help."
   - "This is a big problem for you. How can I help?"
   - "I know it is hard for you to talk now, but I can help you best if you tell me what just happened here."

Showing interest is not only done by saying something. Sometimes what you do can be more important than what you say. Here are some ways through which you might show your interest. Some may not be appropriate in all situations. Use your judgment in applying these techniques.

   - Sit down with the crisis victim.
   - Keep a good posture. Lean forward a bit. Do not slouch in your seat.
   - Face the victim. Use eye contact for communication.
   - Offer a cigarette, candy, food, a blanket, or other appropriate item to the victim.
   - Move a little closer to the victim if he starts talking about emotionally grave topics.
   - *Touch the victim.* Some crisis victims need and accept

18

human contact. Holding someone's hand, or placing a hand on their arm or shoulder, or rubbing the victim's shoulders is fine in some circumstances. This should not be done if the crisis worker feels uncomfortable, or if there is some danger in physical closeness. It is also not a good idea to touch a victim of assault. (See the chapters on violence and sexual assault.)

4. *Listen Carefully.* Do not try to speak when the victim is speaking.

5. *Focus Attention.* Center on the crisis victim and the current situation.

6. *Wait—Think—Respond.* Waiting helps one to think, and thinking increases the chance that the response will be the right one. A short pause is usually all that is necessary.

7. *Repeat.* Do not repeat everything, just the general idea. For example, a depressed patient might say, "My life is a mess. My wife walked out. I'm failing in my job. I don't know what to do." The crisis worker may respond in this way, "A lot of painful things have happened to you lately. You sound lonely and confused." (Notice the substitution of key feeling words, "lonely" and "confused" for the victim's story.)

8. *Sharing of Self.* Sharing a small part of oneself (not the whole life story) can be very helpful to a victim. It makes them feel less alone. For example, a crisis worker trying to confirm child abuse might say to a possible child abusing parent, "Sometimes when my children act up they make me very angry. Does that happen to you with your kids?"

9. *Be Honest.* Nothing hurts a good working relationship more than a lie from the crisis worker. Victims of crisis know when they are being lied to.

10. *Give Hope.* Try to comfort a victim, but do not give false hope in the process. For example, "The fire was very bad, but we were able to contain it to the kitchen and dining room. There is a possibility that most of the furniture in the living room can be salvaged and cleaned."

11. *Observe Physical Energy.* Inactivity implies shock or depression. The quiet, unmoving crisis victim, who is not troublesome to crisis workers, is often in much more

19

> serious emotional trouble than the person who is yelling, crying, and moving. The extremely subdued crisis victim is usually in a state of emotional distress.
>
> 12. *Observe Incongruency.* The person who tells you that he is "just fine" but is crying is probably not fine.
>
> 13. *Suspend Your Frame of Reference.* Try to see the problem through the eyes of the victim. This is just a reminder because it is so important to remember this point.

(The above material was compiled from a number of sources. [1,2,5,6,7,8,9,10])

## E. Characteristics of a Good Communicator

Good communicators:

- Have a good self image.
- Listen intently.
- Express themselves clearly.
- Can cope with strong emotions (their own and others).
- Share bits of themselves.
- Are honest.
- Are empathetic.
- Talk about the here and now issues.
- Are warm.
- Care about people. [5]

## II. INTERVIEWING TECHNIQUES

## A. Information Gathering and Diagnosis

To achieve a proper assessment of a crisis victim, an adequate amount of information must be gathered so that a basic diagnosis of the crisis can be made. Once the diagnosis is made, then it is possible to develop the plan of action which may solve the problem.

Assessment is begun as soon as the call is received. The dispatcher attempts to get answers to as many of the five "W" questions as possible. He wants to know *what* has happened, *where* it happened, *when* it happened, *why* it happened, and to *whom* it happened.

20

The personnel who respond to the scene will try to build on whatever information the dispatcher was able to gather. They will use essentially the same set of questions, but will try for more details.

Crisis workers rely on a variety of information sources. Information sources are:

1. The dispatcher
2. The scene (what is observed)
3. Past experiences
4. The people involved
5. The witnesses
6. Family members
7. The interview
8. Other sources [11,15]

## B. The Interview and Assessment

The crisis interview is simply a conversation designed to gather information about a situation and a person (or people). There is a second purpose to an interview, which is to establish a working relationship with a crisis victim so that the victim will work cooperatively with the rescuer to resolve a problem. [13]

Interviews have four distinct parts. They are usually identified as the:

1. Introduction
2. Transition
3. Process
4. Closure [8]

## 1. Introduction

A. Make a calm, clear, and short statement of who you are and why you are there.
B. Scan the environment to assure yourself that there are no serious dangers or surprises.
C. Begin to organize the crisis scene.
D. Be confident.
E. Take an active role in controlling the situation.

Other hints to make an interview run smoothly:

A. Address the victim with respect. Use the titles "Mr." or "Mrs." with adults.

B. Take up a position that puts you on the same level with the victim (such as sitting or standing).

C. If appropriate, offer your hand for a handshake upon introduction, or take off your cap as you enter someone's house.

D. Explain what you are about to do. For example, "Mrs. King, I need to ask you some questions about this situation. Please do the best you can to give us the information we need to work out a solution."

E. Asking is usually more effective than telling someone something. "May I ask you a few questions?"

F. When appropriate, use the word, "we." It gives an impression that the crisis worker is teaming up with the victim to solve the problem. For example, "I think, if you can explain what happened, we might be able to figure out some way to handle this."

G. Begin the interview where the person happens to be emotionally. For instance, "You seem very upset and angry right now. Can you tell me what happened just before I arrived?"

H. Demonstrate interest. Ways to do this have been described earlier in the chapter. Here are some suggestions about what you might say. "Go ahead, I'm listening," or "I can see how that would upset you."

I. Offer help in a manner that does not imply weakness or mental illness. Instead of saying, "You really can't handle this, can you?," you would be better off saying, "This is a pretty serious problem. I'd like to help you through it. I think we can beat it if we work as a team."

J. Allow the victim to express his emotions.

## 2. Transition

In this part of the interview, the victim will test the crisis worker to see how far he can push before drawing a reaction. The crisis worker may test the victim to see how motivated he might be and how much he is able to help himself. [8]

The crisis worker:

A. Should be careful not to test too much, and

B. He should keep calm control over the situation.

Transition is a short but very important period. It will set up the remainder of the interview or it will destroy it if it is not handled correctly.

One example is the cardiac patient who insists on walking to the ambulance. This is a testing procedure. The ambulance personnel must not be manipulated in this case and should take control, calmly insisting that the victim do as they say because his condition is serious and will not allow for walking around at this time. Another example is the case of a man holding a gun to his head and threatening to kill himself if the crisis worker comes any closer. Testing the victim's intent by coming closer may have the very negative effect of quickly ending the interview!

## 3. Process of the Interview

The process section of an interview is the major portion. Most of the information is obtained during the process and it is in this section that methods of managing the problem are developed. [8,13]

The order in which the information is obtained is not essential. It may be necessary to skip around to get questions answered. The following is the usual order in which information is obtained, and the types of information sought.

A. Identification data:
  - Name
  - Address
  - Age
  - Occupation
  - Marital status
  - Other pertinent information

B. Relationship Data
  - Who is involved?
  - Are they related?
  - Children involved?
  - Who can be called upon to help?
  - Other

C. Nature of the Current Problem
- What is happening now?
- What just occurred?
- When did the problem begin?
- Where did the incident occur?
- Why did it occur?

D. Recent History
- Did anything occur in the family that might upset the members? For example, were there any births, deaths, marriages, separations, moves, divorces, illnesses, or losses of property?
- Any history of alcoholism?
- Any history of emotional problems?
- Is there a history of depression?
- Has this situation occurred before?
- Other pertinent information.

## 4. Closure

The closure is the ending of the interview. It is always necessary. Without closure, victims of crises feel that they have loose ends which have not been tied together. [2,7,8]
Interviewers should:

- Thank the person for cooperating in the interview.
- Give some idea of what will happen next.
- Say goodbye to the person if this is the last step in the helping process.
- Make sure that the necessary information is transferred to the next helping person.

## C. ASSESSMENT AND DIAGNOSIS

The diagnosis is the judgment made by the crisis worker about the information that has been gathered during the interview. It depends on a number of factors. First, the interviewer must decide whether the crisis situation is acute (new) or chronic (over six weeks old).

Secondly, a decision needs to be made about the seriousness of the situation:

Mild—no serious problem.

Moderate—some dangers involved.

Severe—life, or limb-threatening, or the possibility of major psychological damage.

The crisis worker now must decide if the crisis is:

A. Interpersonal—between the victim and others (family problem).

B. Intrapersonal—inside the person (severe depression or psychosis).

C. Situational—such as a fire or flood.

The next item to decide is whether the victim is coping with the problem, or whether he or she needs additional help from outside sources.

Finally, the crisis worker wants to make a decision about the resources, their practicality, and availability.

- Who can help?
- What would help the most now in this crisis?
- Are the people who are named as resources prepared to help?

The diagnosis is based on whether the situation is:

A. A crisis.

B. Mild, moderate, or severe.

C. Interpersonal, intrapersonal, or situational.

D. Is the victim coping adequately?

E. What are the available resources? [15,16]


## D. MAKING THE PLAN OF ACTION

The success of a crisis intervention plan depends heavily on the good working relationship established with the victim during the assessment interview and diagnosis. Crisis victims usually cooperate in creating and implementing a plan only if they feel they can trust the crisis worker.

Crisis planning also depends on the accuracy of the assessment. If the plan does not match the assessment, it will not work.

Crisis intervention plans will work if they are:

- Short term, designed to handle current problems
- Practical
- Immediate—crises cannot wait to be worked on
- Action oriented. Theoretical plans are useless. The crisis plan has to do something.
- Organized
- Planned with the victim's cooperation
- Flexible
- Imaginative
- Resourceful
- Well thought out
- Within the capacities and limitations of the crisis worker (*and* of the victim).
- Include a provision for referral to an appropriate medical, legal, or social agency. [16]

## FINAL STEPS

Of course, the next task for the crisis worker is to implement the plan, and once operating, it is necessary that it be checked periodically. If it is not working, a new plan has to be developed. If it is working, it is maintained until the closure of the intervention.

REFERENCES

1. Johnson DW: Increasing your communications skills. *In* Reaching Out, Interpersonal Effectiveness and Self Actualization. Englewood Cliffs, NJ; Prentice-Hall, 1972
2. Napier RW, Gershenfeld MK: Perception and communication. *In* Groups: Theory and Experience. Boston, Houghton Mifflin Co., 1973
3. Schramm C: Factors affecting the communication process. From unpublished lecture notes. Baltimore County, University of Maryland, Education Department, 1970
4. Maslow AH: Self actualization and beyond. *In* Bugental JFT (ed): Challenges in Humanistic Psychology. New York, McGraw-Hill Book Co., 1967

5. Chartier MR: Five components contributing to effective interpersonal communication. *In* Pfeiffer JW, Jones JE (eds): Annual Handbook for Group Facilitators. LaJolla, CA; University Associates Publishers Co., 1974
6. Jourard SM: The Transparent Self. New York, Van Nostrand Reinhold Co., 1971
7. Carkhuff R: The Art of Helping. Amherst, MA; Human Resource Development Press, 1972
8. Koopman EJ, Hunt EJ, Corvan SD: Talking Together. Kalamazoo, MI; Behaviordelio, Inc., 1978
9. Egan G: Interpersonal Living: A Skills/Contract Approach to Human-Relations Training In Groups. Monterey, CA; Brooks/Cole Publishing Co., 1976
10. Mill C, Porter LC (eds): Reading Book for Laboratories in Human Relations Training. Arlington, VA; NTL Institute for Applied Behavioral Science, 1972
11. Gazzaniga AB, Iseri L, Boren M: Emergency Care: Principles and Practices for the EMT-Paramedic. Reston, VA; Reston Publishing Co., 1979
12. Grant H, Murray R: Emergency Care, 2nd ed. Bowie, MD; Robert J. Brady Co., 1978
13. Sundberg ND: Assessment of Persons. Englewood Cliffs, NJ; Prentice-Hall, Inc., 1977
14. The Committee on Allied Health, American Academy of Orthopedic Surgeons: Emergency Care and Transportation of the Sick and Injured, 2nd ed. Menasha, WI; George Banta Co., Inc., 1977
15. Bard M: The Function of the Police in Crisis Intervention and Conflict Management. Washington, DC; United States Department of Justice, Law Enforcement Assistance Administration, National Institute of Law Enforcement and Criminal Justice, 1975
16. Parad HJ (ed): Crisis Intervention: Selected Readings. New York, Family Service Association of America, 1965

CHAPTER **3**

# Legal Aspects of Crisis Intervention

Jeffrey T. Mitchell, M.S.

## INTRODUCTION

It would be foolish for an emergency service worker to operate without some basic understanding of the legal implications of such work. This comment applies especially to personnel who function in crisis situations. Circumstances may change quickly during crises and crisis workers must always be alert to their legal limitations.

It is possible that a crisis worker can be sued. (Any person may sue any other for practically any reason.) It is important that crisis workers be aware of this potential and avoid making statements or behaving in a manner that could become grounds for legal action.

This chapter will provide a set of general principles regarding law, the legal limitations, and liabilities which affect emergency service personnel. It will provide pertinent information on such topics as negligence, assault and battery, crisis victim rights, report writing, and the involuntary commitment of a mentally disturbed person to a psychiatric center.

A word of caution is in order. The contents of this chapter are simple broad statements regarding law, and they should not be considered definitive. Laws vary from jurisdiction to jurisdiction. It is not possible to cover here every conceivable legal circumstance. Emergency service personnel are urged to become familiar with the laws which affect their work within their own jurisdictions. Should they need more detailed legal advice, they should contact their state's attorney's office or a private lawyer.

## COMMON LEGAL PROBLEMS ENCOUNTERED
## IN CRISIS INTERVENTION

Crisis workers are most likely to encounter the following types of legal problems:

- Violations of motor vehicle laws.
- Vehicular accidents (while operating emergency apparatus).
- Property damage.
- Legal complications related to the care of the victim.
    A. By commission (something they did).
    B. By omission (something they did not do, but should have done). [1]


## WHO MUST ACT IN A CRISIS

Generally speaking, people are not required by law to help one another. Morals and a code of ethics may motivate them to help but they cannot be legislated to do so. There are some exceptions, however, and these people have a duty to help others under certain conditions. The exceptions are police officers, firefighters, and emergency medical personnel. In some states, certain professionals, such as doctors and nurses, have also been designated to help others because of the special nature of their professions. Practically all states, which require certain helping activities from designated people, have established legal immunity for these people.

Legal immunity is usually covered under the "Good Samaritan Laws." A Good Samaritan law provides legal protection from liability for emergency service personnel and others who provide reasonable and prudent care to people. The reasonable and prudent care, however, has to be administered according to a set of previously established criteria. Good Samaritan laws cut down substantially on the possibility of legal involvement for emergency service workers. Therefore, they should not hesitate to aid people who need their help. If they use common sense and follow established criteria, the chances of being sued are quite small. [2]

## CRITERIA FOR INTERVENTION

Whenever a person is required to help another according to a certain defined method, he is being required to follow a Standard of Care (or Operation). A standard of care is somewhat flexible because it may change as circumstances change. Most standards of care are established according to local custom, ordinances, administrative orders, or laws. *A standard of care is the usual manner in which an individual is expected to act.* It covers such things as the splinting of fractures by ambulance personnel before moving an accident victim, and the investigation of a suspected child abuse situation by police officers.

One common standard of care, which has become a general principle of law, deals with the concept of abandonment. A person who begins to intervene in a crisis is obligated to continue the intervention, once he has initiated it, unless a more qualified person relieves him. To stop helping someone once he has started the care, without providing for continued care, means that he has "abandoned" the patient and he is liable for any damages suffered by the victim as a result of his abandonment.

Another common standard of operation, which is particularly relevant for police officers, is that a person's civil rights will not be limited except by due process of law. Arresting a person prior to a proper investigation, or adequate suspicion of a criminal act usually constitutes a violation of this standard. [3,4]

## NEGLIGENCE

When a person, with a duty to act or behave in a certain manner, fails to conform to the set standards, he is considered negligent and is responsible for any resulting injury sustained by the victim from his actions. For example, if a police officer uses his night stick against another person in a manner that is not prescribed by normal police training and practice, he may be considered negligent and responsible for damages. A paramedic would be liable, in most instances, if he refused to follow the reasonable and prudent orders of a physician who was responsible for the care of the patient.

It is also possible to be held liable for the actions of another which result in further injury to a crisis victim. An example would be the failure to report to a superior that one's partner arrived for work in an intoxicated state. Should the intoxicated person perform actions that further injure or threaten a crisis victim, he, as well as his partner who failed to report the problem, would be negligent and liable for damages. [2]

The concept of negligence raises many doubts and concerns for emergency service personnel. Although some concern is justifiable, it should not be exaggerated. Charges of negligence are usually only filed if a person is injured by the actions of a crisis worker. Secondly, the victim must prove that the crisis worker acted with a blatant disregard for proper procedures. An error in judgment is usually not considered negligent. If the crisis worker can demonstrate that he acted in a prudent and reasonable manner under the circumstances, it is highly unlikely that he will be found negligent. [5]

## CONFIDENTIALITY

Every person has a right to privacy. This is a standard that is upheld by tradition as well as law. The crisis victim's records are confidential. Unauthorized and unnecessary discussion of the incident, in which the victim was involved, especially regarding details of a confidential nature, is a violation of a standard of good care and leaves emergency service personnel open for suit. The only discussions which should take place are those which are necessary for the treatment, transportation, and continued care of the victim. It is most important to keep confidential identifying information such as the name, address, and phone number of a victim. [2,6]

## ASSAULT AND BATTERY

Part of the patient's right to privacy also protects him from being touched by others without his consent. If an emergency service worker touches a crisis victim without first obtaining the person's permission, he has committed a battery (the "unlawful physical touching of another without the other party's consent"). [5] If a crisis worker threatens violence or performs an act of violence against a victim, he then commits an assault ("unlawfully placing another in apprehension of immediate bodily harm without his consent"). [5] Both criminal and civil charges may be placed against the crisis worker for assault and battery. Assault and battery charges cannot be brought against a person who was acting in his own self defense as long as he did not utilize unreasonable and excessive force.

Emergency service personnel also have a right and a duty to use reasonable and necessary force to prevent a person from hurting himself or other people. They may therefore restrain (with the proper equipment) a person or imprison him if he presents a clear and imminent danger to himself or others. Charges of assault and battery would not be upheld under these circumstances. [1,5]

Crisis workers are generally required to use appropriate restraining equipment such as padded restraints, wide straps, or bands of cloth. The use of wire and chains is not usually acceptable and leaves emergency personnel vulnerable to suits for damages.

General standards of care require that adequate personnel be on hand to subdue a person who becomes violent and uncontrolled. The term "adequate personnel" can mean different things under different circumstances. However, three or four people are typically needed to subdue a violent person. Emergency service personnel would be unwise, both from a safety point of view and from a legal point of view, to attempt to subdue an uncontrolled and dangerous person with less than three or four personnel. The assistance of police officers is usually relied upon in most cases. [5]

## CONSENT

A person may not bring suit for assault and battery charges if he has given his permission for another to touch and/or treat him.

Any person who is an adult (over 18 in most states) may refuse the care and treatment of crisis workers as long as he is in control of his faculties (mind and behavior). This is part of the standard which protects a person's privacy.

It is always better to have a person's consent before touching or treating him. Consent provides a strong protection against being sued.

There are two major types of consent. The first is called *actual* and means that a person, either verbally or by his actions, expresses a desire to be touched, examined, and treated by emergency personnel. This consent may be written or verbal and it must be an informed consent. The person must have the proper information and a sufficient mental and physical capacity to make a proper decision. [1,3]

The other type of consent is *implied* consent. This applies to situations in which the crisis victim is unconscious and unable to give proper consent. It is appropriate to proceed in giving care and treatment in such a case because the law holds that a person in his right mind would want care and treatment under the circumstances. However, only that touching or care which is absolutely necessary to preserve life, prevent further injury, or psychological disruption is allowed. An emergency condition must exist. The emergency condition is one in which there is a risk of death, physical impairment, or a serious deterioration of a person's present condition. In an emergency situation, a spouse or close relative may give consent for the victim. [1,3,5,6]

In the case of children under 17 years of age, parents must usually give consent for touching and treatment. In an emergency, consent is implied as in the adult case. People have a legal right to refuse interventions by crisis workers for religious reasons. To proceed to touch or treat someone, even a child, against such objections makes one liable.

The right to refuse care has been upheld many times. It is important that the refusal be an informed one. Crisis workers have a duty to inform the refusing party of the possible dangers of such a refusal. If possible, a refusal form should be signed by the person or parent.

If there is any doubt as to whether a crisis worker should treat or not treat a particular case, he would do well to render the treatment. *Failure to act in a crisis carries a greater legal liability than acting in favor of the treatment.* [3]


## EMERGENCY COMMITMENT TO A PSYCHIATRIC HOSPITAL

A person in a severe emotional crisis can be admitted to a psychiatric center in one of two ways in most states. He may voluntarily present himself to that psychiatric center or to a hospital emergency room for evaluation. If he demonstrates sufficient emotional disturbance during the evaluation, he may be admitted for psychiatric treatment. Usually, one or two physicians must certify that the person is emotionally disturbed. The person may sign himself out of the psychiatric center within a reasonable period of time if he so chooses.

An involuntary admission is accomplished in much the

same way except that other people, usually the person's family, bring the person in for evaluation. Frequently, the police may have to be called to subdue and transport the person. Again, one or two physicians must examine the person and sign certifying statements that the person is mentally disturbed and is likely to cause harm to himself or others. Some states require a legal hearing before involuntary admission can take place. The patient must remain in the psychiatric center for a longer period of time and must be re-evaluated before being released. In such cases, the police are usually delegated the task of transporting mentally disturbed people to the psychiatric center. [4,6]

## REPORT WRITING

Reports involving emotional crises need to be carefully written. It is impossible to predict the course of such cases and the written record is the best protection should there be any legal involvement in the future. The written record should include notes written at the time of, or shortly after, the incident. They must be factual, clear, concise, and legible. Personal opinions should be kept out completely. Only widely used and understood abbreviations should be utilized. The written record is most often used in court as testimony in assault cases, child abuse, and in cases involving charges of negligence on the part of the crisis worker. Notes should be written with the thought in mind that they may be used in a future court case. [2]

## REPORTING REQUIREMENTS

Emergency personnel are required to report various things in different states. Child abuse is something that must be reported to the police or social service agencies in practically all states. Some states require the reporting of suicide attempts, drug abuse, dog bites, communicable diseases, assaults and rapes, births, and deaths. Felonies must always be reported. It is a good idea for crisis workers to be familiar with incidents in their own jurisdictions which must be reported by them and to whom they are to be reported. [3]

## SEARCHING FOR IDENTIFICATION OR MEDICAL INFORMATION

In situations involving unconscious or incapacitated patients, it is frequently necessary to search through that person's personal effects to find identification or medical information. This is usually allowed as long as the search is limited to the purposes stated above. For one's own protection, crisis workers should have at least one, and possibly two, witnesses from among their colleagues as they search through someone's personal effects.

## OTHER LEGAL RESPONSIBILITIES

Crisis workers are required to preserve a crime scene. If they must move something to get to a victim they should mentally note its exact position before moving it (or chalk mark the spot).

Crisis workers may not legally "pronounce" someone dead. However, if death has obviously taken place, they may tell family members that the victim is dead and that there is nothing further anyone can do to save that person's life. [1,2]

## CONCLUSION

There are two basic ingredients which are commonly present in law suits. The first is that the person bringing suit was injured, physically or psychologically. The second ingredient is that there was a breakdown in communication. These pitfalls can be easily avoided if crisis workers are well trained and function within their capacities and limitations, and if they treat people as human beings and not just as cases. [2]

### REFERENCES

1. Grant H, Murray R: The EMT and the law. *In* Grant H, Murray R (eds): Emergency Care, 2nd ed. Bowie MD; Robert J. Brady Co., 1978
2. Rozovsky LE: Answers to the 15 legal questions nurses usually ask. Nursing, July, 1978
3. The Committee on Allied Health. Legal Responsibilities. *In*

Emergency Care and Transportation of the Sick and Injured, 2nd ed. Menasha, WI; George Banta Co., Inc., 1977

4. Kolb C: Psychiatry and the Law. *In* Modern Clinical Psychiatry, 9th ed. Philadelphia, W. B. Saunders Company, 1977

5. George JE (ed): Psychiatric Emergencies. *In* Emergency Medical Technician Legal Bulletin, Vol. 3, No. 3. Westville, New Jersey; Med/ Law Publishers, Inc., Summer 1979.

6. Ruben DD: Legal aspects of mental health emergencies. *In* Resnik HLP, Ruben (eds): Emergency Care, the Management of Mental Health Crises. Bowie, MD; The Charles Press, Inc., 1975

# CHAPTER 4

# The Management of Acute Emotional Disturbances

Lawrence D. Messier, M.A.

## INTRODUCTION

One of the most confusing situations for crisis workers is an incident involving an emotionally disturbed person. The apprehension felt by crisis workers is due in part to some mistaken beliefs about the emotionally disturbed. For example, many people believe that emotional disturbance is contagious. Many think that if one member of a family is emotionally disturbed, other members of the family are also disturbed. This is not true. One person's emotional illness does not necessarily cause disturbance in others. Another misconception is that the emotionally disturbed individual is a "time bomb" waiting to explode. In fact, most emotionally disturbed people are withdrawn and afraid. Violent outbursts do occur but the "psychopathic killer" is more often seen in movies than in the real world.

However, the crisis worker's concern about dealing with emotionally disturbed individuals is not totally unfounded. The disturbed person often exhibits behavior that is inappropriate and difficult to understand. Communication with such individuals is difficult and they do not always respond to the helpful efforts of crisis workers.

As previously mentioned in Chapter One, crisis workers will deal with few seriously disturbed people, and most of these individuals will pose no danger to the crisis worker. Most will welcome assistance since they are unable to cope with the crisis situation by themselves.

This chapter will provide the information and guidelines for intervention which will enable the crisis worker to intervene in a confident and successful manner.

## DEFINITIONS

1. *Anxiety*—a feeling of dread and nervousness about the future without a specific cause for that feeling. [1]

2. *Delusion*—a false belief which cannot be changed by reasoning or demonstration of facts to the contrary. For example, the person believes he is dying.

3. *Hallucination*—a false perception, the acceptance of images and sensations *from within the individual* as if they existed in reality. An example is the hearing of voices or the seeing of dream-like images. [1]

4. *Illusion*—a mistaken or distorted perception, as in seeing a branch as a snake. An illusion is similar to a hallucination except the object exists in reality, but is misinterpreted by the person's mind.

## BACKGROUND

Any discussion of emotional disturbance must occur within the framework of human behavior in general. The diagram below re-

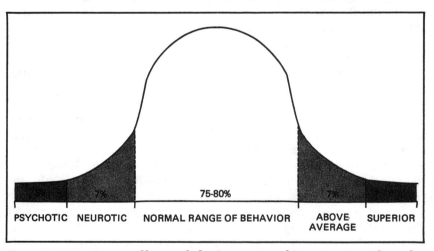

*Figure 4.1   Continuum of human behavior measured in percentage of population.*

veals the place of disturbed behavior (neurotic and psychotic) in respect to all of human behavior (see Figure 4.1).

As previously mentioned in Chapter One, psychotic (severely disturbed) individuals are a relatively small part of the population. Neurotics, or moderately disturbed people, represent a somewhat larger percentage than psychotics, but are still a rather small part of the total population. Therefore, crisis situations involving seriously disturbed individuals are not likely to occur too frequently. [2,4]

The behavior of a seriously disturbed person is not always bizarre and uncontrolled. Such individuals may appear normal in some of their behavior patterns. The personality traits and behaviors of disturbed people are more extreme, more inappropriate, and more maladaptive than displays of the same traits and behaviors seen in most normal persons. [2]

Specific causes of most emotional disorders have not yet been determined. Research suggests that many factors such as genetics, social factors, chemical imbalances in the body, child rearing, and stress all seem to be related to emotional disturbance. [2,3]

The following section will discuss the three major classes or groups of emotional disorders. The information presented here will aid the crisis worker in understanding and helping the emotionally disturbed person. Specific diagnosis should be left to qualified mental health professionals.


## TRANSIENT OR SITUATIONAL DISORDERS

This group of emotional disorders is the least severe of the three groups. As the name implies, the disturbance is usually temporary and is likely to occur under conditions of prolonged or overwhelming stress. In situations such as terrifying accidents, severe physical injury or a disaster, emotional disorders may develop even in people who have stable personalities. The onset may be sudden, as in accident or injury situations, or it may be gradual when caused by constant exposure to a high degree of stress as in the "burnout" syndrome (see Chapter 15). The individual, with therapeutic help, usually recovers completely once the stressful situation is resolved. [4]

The behavior of an individual who is experiencing this temporary form of emotional disturbance will be very similar or identical to the behavior of the neurotic, and even psychotic, forms of emotional disturbance. The only difference is that the disturbance is temporary, and rapid, total recovery usually follows. [3,4]

## NEUROSIS

This form of emotional disturbance is not as severe as the psychotic disturbance and may be experienced to some degree by most people at some point in their lives. It is experienced as an unpleasant emotional state of nervousness, tension, and apprehension. The neurotic individual wants to enjoy life and be happy, but is hindered by unknown fears, doubts, guilt, and feelings of inferiority. The central feature of neurosis is the almost constant presence of anxiety. There are no hallucinations, delusions, or bizarre behavior which is seen in psychosis. Neurotic symptoms reduce the efficiency of the individual and cause great anguish, but do not necessarily prevent him from functioning normally in his job, relationships with others, and everyday activities. In short, the neurotic is normal in most ways, but is anxious and worried. The neurotic recognizes his symptoms as a problem, but is unable to change this behavior. [2,3,4] Most neurotic people do not fit into a precise pattern and will show a combination of the symptom patterns listed below. [3,4]

1. *Anxiety*—Anxiety involves a general feeling of nervousness and impending disaster with no apparent reason for such feelings. Anxiety is usually identified by poor concentration, irritability, sleep disturbances, and nightmares. The anxiety is most visible in anxiety attacks which can occur at any time. These attacks are marked by:

- Cardiac palpitation and irregularity
- Breathlessness or hyperventilation
- Feelings of weakness
- Hand tremors
- Nausea
  (No physical causes can be associated with these symptoms.)

2. *Depression*—Anxiety is present and combined with feelings of dejection, helplessness, hopelessness, and guilt. The person feels he is a failure, and loses interest in previous activities and friends.

3. *Phobias*—This pattern is marked by intense and illogical fears of specific objects or situations. The individual, in the face of the fearful object or situation, experiences feelings of apprehension, palpitations, nausea, faintness and, if escape is not immediate, will react with panic. Some common phobias are:

- Acrophobia—fear of high places
- Claustrophobia—fear of closed places
- Hematophobia—fear of blood
- Ochlophobia—fear of crowds

4. *Other symptom patterns of neurosis include:*

- Paralysis
- Deafness
- Blindness
- Recurring dreams
- Repetitive thoughts
- Repeated actions (hand washing)
- Constant fatigue
- Aches and pains
- Hazy thinking
- Worry over health

## PSYCHOSIS

Psychosis is the most severe form of emotional disturbance. It involves severe disruption of thought processes, emotions, and one's sense of time and place. The psychotic individual is usually unable to accomplish everyday tasks such as holding a job and relating to other people. His emotional expressions are often extreme and the psychotic does not recognize that his behavior is abnormal. In most cases, the behavior of the psychotic individual is so unusual that it will be immediately apparent to the crisis worker. [1,4,5]

Although there are several distinctive forms of psychosis, the primary task of the crisis worker is to determine how severely the person is disturbed. The following symptoms of psychosis are outlined to aid in recognizing the seriously disturbed individual. These symptoms are displayed by most psychotics and should immediately alert the crisis worker to the presence of serious emotional disturbance. [3,4]

*1. Disorganized Thinking.*

- Disorientation—The psychotic may not be able to determine the time of day, day of the week, or even the year. He may not be aware of his current location or how he got there. The individual may not be able to recall personal information, such as birthdate, age, address, or names of family members.
- Inattention—The psychotic is often in a state of confusion and has great difficulty focusing attention on one topic. He may jump from one subject to another quickly and frequently. The ideas of the psychotic are not logically associated with one another and may not make sense.
- Loss of control over behavior—The use of profanity, sexual advances, and unprovoked verbal or physical attacks are common examples of this loss of control.

*2. Delusions*—These false beliefs will be rigidly maintained despite their absurdity or evidence to the contrary. Some examples are:

- Guilt over committing some unpardonable sin.
- Having a dreaded serious disease.
- Persecution (other people are plotting against him or manipulating him in some secret or mysterious way).
- The individual believes he is some important person who is to save the world from some evil.

*3. Hallucinations*—The hearing of voices or seeing of images which do not exist in reality. Some common hallucinations are:

- Hearing voices which talk to or about the individual; the person believes the voices are talking in a derogatory way or instructing him to perform some act.
- Tasting poison in food or feeling insects under the skin.
- Communicating with famous figures such as Abraham Lincoln.

*4. Emotional Extremeness*—extremes may be in either direction; lack of emotional responsiveness or excessive emotionality such as:

- Apathetic and emotionally unresponsive.
- Wildly euphoric, elated, ecstatic.

- Severely depressed, withdrawn, detached.
- Inappropriate emotions such as laughter at the death of a loved one, or sadness in response to a joyful event.

5. *Disturbance of Motor Behavior*—the loss of ability to perform goal-directed movements in an ordered manner.

- Difficulty initiating activities.
- Maintaining a fixed posture for long periods of time, as if frozen in the middle of an action.
- Continuous repetition of speech or physical acts.
- Overactivity, constant pacing, crying, hand-wringing.

## AGGRESSIVE BEHAVIOR AND EMOTIONAL DISTURBANCE

The potential for aggressive response from emotionally disturbed individuals is minimal in most situations. Despite the generally low potential for violent behavior, the presence of certain factors does greatly increase the chances for aggressive behavior. The presence of any of these factors listed below, should alert the crisis worker to the possibility of violent behavior. In such cases, the crisis worker should proceed with caution and alert additional personnel.

1. Alcohol—See Chapter Seven
2. Addictive substances—See Chapter Eight
3. Hallucination and delusions—In some cases, disturbed individuals will respond to these hallucinations or delusions as if directed to engage in violent behavior.
4. Frustration—Overactive, agitated individuals may react aggressively at attempts to interrupt or frustrate them. The use of restraints or threats may trigger violent responses. [6]

## ASSESSMENT

Assessment of the emotionally disturbed person is not too difficult, but requires good observational and interpersonal skills. The crisis worker must determine the presence or absence of serious emotional disturbance (psychosis) and the potential for aggressive behavior. An assessment can be made by interacting with the individual and observing his responses and behavior.

45

1. Speech
   - Uncommunicative, unresponsive to crisis worker
   - Speech extremely slow or extremely fast
   - Quick and frequent change of topic
   - Speech unrelated to present situation
   - Use of strange words, disorganized, illogical conversation

2. Mood—This may be obvious, but can be elicited by asking, "How do you feel?"
   - Severely depressed, intensely quiet, suicidal thoughts
   - Overactive, extreme agitation, constant movement, excessive elation
   - Quick and severe mood changes
   - Emotion inappropriate to situation

3. Alertness
   - Confusion, inability to concentrate or focus on topic
   - Unaware of people and surroundings
   - Loss of awareness of time, place, person

4. Thought
   - Illogical, talks to self
   - Hallucinations
   - Delusions

## INTERVENTION

Successful intervention will depend primarily on the attitude and behavior of crisis workers. Although the individual and the situation may seem absurd, remember the disturbed individual is in a state of crisis and cannot cope alone. The crisis worker can best approach the situation with a nonjudgmental, non-confronting attitude. The crisis worker's ability to communicate caring and acceptance, in as gentle a manner as possible, is most important. It will be helpful to proceed along the following guidelines.

*Step 1*—Make the immediate environment safe and remove sources of stress or provocation. This includes other people. *Reducing stress is crucial.*

*Step 2*—Attempt to establish communication with the individual. The focus should be on building trust. Do this by:

- Sincerely communicating your desire to help.
- Gently attempting to get the individual to respond to you. The individual's responses will help in assessing the situation.
- Responding with understanding to the individual's feelings.

*Step 3*—Assess the degree of emotional disturbance and potential for aggressive behavior.

*Step 4*—Continue intervention by doing the following:

## A. For Mild Emotional Disturbance

- Continue to respond with understanding.
- Attempt to focus on problems identified by the individual.
- Confidently, but realistically, consider solutions to the problem(s).
- Consider, with the individual, possible referrals (physicians, mental health workers).
- If no referral is available, consider temporary hospitalization.

## B. For Severe Disturbance or High Aggressive Potential

- Prepare the patient as gently as possible for the trip to the hospital.
- Attempt to get him to voluntarily accept hospitalization. Proceed to the hospital and stay with the person until appropriate hospital personnel can take over.
- If the individual refuses voluntary hospitalization, call for support.
- Restraint and force should be used only as a last resort.

47

*DO NOT*

1. Threaten the individual or tell him that he is crazy or ridiculous.
2. Draw weapons unless there is an immediate threat to the life of someone involved. Provocation may evoke violent responses in emotionally disturbed people.
3. Display restraint equipment unless there is no other alternative. This also may provoke violent behavior.
4. "Play along" with delusions and hallucinations of the individual. This also may incite unpredictable behavior on his part. [3,5,6]

## REFERENCES

1. Chaplin P: Dictionary of Psychology. New York, Dell Publishing Company, 1975
2. Page D: Psychopathology: The Science of Understanding Deviance. Chicago, Aldine Publishing Company, 1975
3. Freedman AM, Kaplan HI, Saddock BJ: Modern Synopsis of Comprehensive Textbook of Psychiatry, II. Baltimore, Williams and Wilkins, 1976
4. Coleman C: Psychology and Effective Behavior. Glenview, IL; Scott, Foresman and Company, 1969
5. Kolb C: Noyes' Modern Clinical Psychiatry. Philadelphia, W. B. Saunders, 1968
6. Rees WLL: A Short Textbook of Psychiatry. Philadelphia, Lippincott, 1976

CHAPTER **5**

# Responding to a Home Emergency

Margaret M. Epperson-Sebour, M.S.W.

Historically, family emergencies were resolved within the family structure. Prior to the enormous growth of industry in the US, families appeared to be more self-sufficient. They relied on an extended network of family members to provide many of the basic functions that have since been taken over by social service agencies.

Today, US citizens view health care and protection as an entitlement, and the government is mandated to see that these services are provided. Even emergency service personnel are called upon to meet family needs that were once provided by the family itself. Meeting these needs can be a difficult and challenging task.

Characteristically, the modern, mobile American family lacks the support of parents, relatives, and childhood friends, and must rely on public services when an emergency strikes the family. Therefore, emergency services personnel must bear the burden of assisting these families and providing or obtaining the emergency assistance needed.

The purpose of this chapter is to present some guidelines for crisis workers when faced with the task of intervening in common family crisis events. Although there are similarities, no two human situations are identical. The intervention outcome depends on the skill, compassion, and personality of the helping person. A "cook-book" or "how-to" approach to family crisis situations is not appropriate. The general framework presented here can provide a systematic approach when attempting to be helpful.

In attempting to assist families in an emergency, those called to help must learn to *respond* to the situation, not merely *react* blindly or instinctively to it. To *respond* means that one needs to plan, act, and be accountable for his behavior in that situation.

When families are under the stress of a crisis, the helping person must take the responsibility for providing the structure and support the family needs to regain its equilibrium. Usually families in crisis are not acting responsibly. They often can only react instinctively to what has happened.[1] The crisis worker must organize his approach to the situation so that his intervention is effective in helping the family to cope with the crisis.

## DUAL ACTION APPROACH

### I. Situation Action

In responding to a family emergency, one must be prepared to handle not only the family's problem but, also oneself in that particular situation. To do this the crisis worker should take a *Dual Action* approach. *What you do* in a given *SITUATION* and how that particular *SITUATION* affects *YOU* determines the outcome of your response to a family's call for assistance.

The *ACTION is DUAL* because it considers the *helping person* in response to the *crisis situation* involving other people. Under stress both the helping person and the crisis situation need particular attention.

In approaching the SITUATION the crisis worker must:

A —Assess
C —Control
T —Treat
I —Inform
O —Okay
N —Notate

Regarding himself in the situation, the helper must check his own PERSONAL:

A —Attitudes
C —Concern
T —Thinking Ability
I —Interactions
O —Objectivity
N —Needs

What does the *DUAL ACTION* mean? It means that you have an organized and systematic plan of intervention that will expedite a resolution to the crisis.

When called to intervene in a family situation you should:

| | |
|---|---|
| **A—ASSESS** | It is important that your assessment take in the whole scene: Who—What—When—Where. |
| • Who? | Who are the persons actually involved? Who are the persons there but not apparently involved? Who needs to be further involved? Who there can be of assistance if needed? |
| • What? | What actually happened and how did it happen? What seems to be the cause(s)? |
| • When? | When did the event take place? |
| • Where? | Where did the event happen? Where should uninvolved persons go? Where should treatment take place? |

It is important to know "What" actually happened. A crisis worker must not assume anything. It is necessary to get first hand information from those involved or from witnesses. In assessing the "Where," do not overlook the physical structure and interior plan of the dwelling. Crisis workers need to determine and plan an "escape route" for themselves in case one is needed.

| | |
|---|---|
| **C—CONTROL** | The First Responder must place himself in a position of command and give directions. |

Getting control of a confusing and emotional situation can be very difficult. You may need help. Utilize those people who you think will be the most able to assist you. Put them in charge of controlling certain people in the family who are disruptive. If there is no help available, begin with the most disruptive person or persons and assign them direct, simple tasks to be performed out of the immediate area. "I need you to watch the children in the bedroom," or "I need you to get a bucket of hot water," or "I need you to watch for the ambulance/police/doctor, etc. and show them where we are."

If you need to control a large crowd, try to place yourself on a step or on some higher level and give brief information about what has happened and specific forceful directions. For example, stand on the top step of the entryway where you are visible to all and announce in a loud voice, "There has been a shooting inside and we need to get a stretcher in here. Please clear this area so the ambulance crew can work. Okay everybody, step back about ten feet. You people in the back, move back a little so the people here can give us a little room. Come on, a little bit more. That's good. Thank you." Use your arms and hands to direct the crowd. Always be alert for persons in the group willing to help with crowd control. Neighborhood groups, ethnic, and other social groups are more likely to take direction from one of their own than from an outsider. [2]

| | |
|---|---|
| **T—TREAT** | Appropriate treatment must be given as soon as possible. Medical emergencies require immediate evaluation of the injuries or illness and life saving action. Marital conflict needs some kind of arbitration. Disorderly conduct may require arrest. Suicide threats need to be "talked down." Psychotic persons often need restraints and immediate transportation to a hospital. An excessive intake of drugs and/or alcohol often requires immediate medical assistance. Victims of rape, child, or spouse abuse need a sympathetic response to the emotional trauma, physical examination, and medical treatment. |

The procedures and protocols already established by local authorities for the management of emergency situations must be followed. This chapter only refers to guidelines for managing emotional crisis within the context of normal protocols.

| | |
|---|---|
| **I—INFORM** | It is necessary for the crisis worker to inform family members about what needs to be done and how one will do it or help the family to do it. Information helps to relieve stress and families are entitled to know your plan of action. [3] |

52

Families in crisis do not always hear what is said.

- Be brief, clear, and repetitive when communicating with these families.
- Have at least one family member repeat what you have said to make sure that your information has been understood.

O—OKAY    The crisis worker is the one who will bring relief to the immediate situation. Through a systematic, organized approach to the family crisis, the helping person conveys the nonverbal message that competent help has arrived and things will be taken care of. The family receives the message that it is okay to let someone else take over now.

Okaying does not mean that everything will turn out all right. It does mean that someone now is in control and able to act to help resolve the family situation.

- Crisis workers should guard against giving families false hope by saying, "don't worry, everything will be fine." No one can guarantee that.
- In okaying it is best to say something like, "We will do everything we can to help your husband/child/wife," or, "We will stabilize him/her as best we can here then transport him/her to the hospital for further care."

N—NOTATE    A log of calls answered and the collection of certain basic data is required of all crisis workers. It is advisable to note the events which took place from the time of your arrival on the scene until you completed your intervention.

Keeping a brief record enables one to evaluate how effective his intervention was in the situation.

## II. PERSONAL ACTION

When responding to any human situation a person brings with him his own frame of reference (see Chapter Two). One's values, prejudices, goals, mind-set, and economic status are brought to the emergency scene. Crisis workers must learn to use themselves to their greatest advantage in the situation. [4] To do this, they need to look at themselves in the situation and examine their own:

A—ATTITUDES An attitude is the way one thinks and feels about a given situation. A professional response requires a professional attitude of openness, calmness, competency, and compassion.

A professional attitude requires that one be able to consciously put aside preconceived ideas and prejudices about a particular situation. One's personal beliefs about a given race, a particular socio-economic group, substance abusers, and other groups are not always appropriate to a professional response. [5]

C—CONCERN Concern and caring require an awareness of the other's needs and a willingness to meet these needs.

If the emergency service personnel are truly concerned about what has happened to a family, it will be shown by their attitudes, manners, and communications. Those who view calls for help from other people in trouble as an "imposition" on their time will often receive a hostile reaction from family members.

T—THINKING-ABILITY In any situation, a helper must have the capacity to predict with some accuracy what impact actions will have on others involved in the event. A crisis worker should think how his actions will affect both fellow helpers and the people he is attempting to assist.

Good thinking in a crisis requires a calm, clear analysis of the event itself and the emotions which the family members may be experiencing.

I—INTERACTIONS Interactions are the verbal or nonverbal messages which are used between individuals or groups, and which influences the behavior of others. Some styles of interacting can make a situation worse.

54

Crisis workers should check their interactions by asking themselves the following questions: Do you begin to shout orders before a proper assessment is made? Are you too timid and lack assertiveness? Crisis workers must be assertive or firm in order to establish and maintain control. Are you too aggressive? Excessive aggression can engender hostility, even violence, and make your task more difficult.

O—OBJECTIVITY  To be objective in the situation, personnel must learn to keep an open mind when responding to a call. The crisis worker usually has few facts when entering a family situation. It is easy to draw conclusions based only on assumptions about what has happened. Acting on assumptions is risky because it is easy to misread what has happened and initiates an inappropriate plan of action. Objectivity also requires that the crisis worker avoid taking sides and maintain an objective position that permits him to be open and accessible to all family members. [5]

Human problems do not usually have a single "cause-effect" relationship. Most human situations are the result of multiple causes. Many families have had pre-existing problems that contributed to the current crisis. Crisis workers should listen to how each person involved perceives the situation. After listening objectively, they are better equipped to make a more accurate assessment and develop an appropriate treatment plan. [5]

N—NEEDS  Emergency service personnel have a tough and often thankless job. Everyone develops specific needs for job satisfaction and appreciation from peers and supervisors. Personnel who go too long without recognizing and satisfying at least some of those needs are in jeopardy of burning out (see Chapter 15).

## OTHER INTERVENTION TECHNIQUES

Some guidelines for working with families have been suggested earlier in this chapter. Further guidelines are presented here:

- During a family crisis, young children should be removed from the scene and placed under the care of a familiar adult, or older brother or sister, who can provide a sense of security.
- If no one is available to care for young children, they should be placed in an out of the way position, but where they can see or at least hear the parent or guardian.
- Interview those involved in the crisis separately.
- Do not take sides.
- Use a calm, even tone of voice.
- Be careful. Families, in which two or more people are fighting among themselves, will often band together when emergency service personnel arrive and may attack the crisis workers.
- Once fighting members are separated from each other, they should be kept apart long enough to calm down so that they can avoid more fighting.
- Be cautious in touching family members. They may turn on you if they perceive your touch as an attack. Jealousy is also intense in disrupted families. A jealous husband might injure or kill a crisis worker who pays too much attention to his wife.
- Try to get at least one person in the family to work with you. Usually, if one starts to cooperate, other family members follow that lead. Work with the one who seems the most "together."
- Use restraints sparingly. If they must be used, they should be applied quickly. Explain why it was necessary to restrain only after the restraints are on properly. Do not remove the restraints until the person is under adequate care by hospital personnel. [1, 4, 5, 6]

56

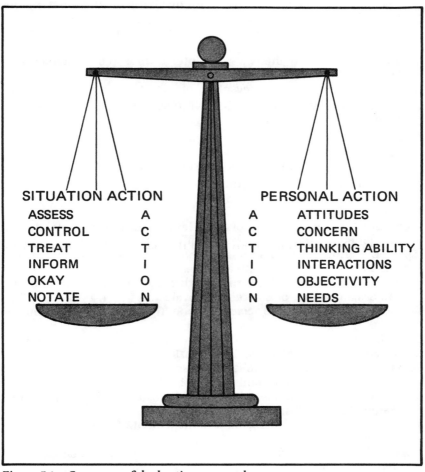

*Figure 5.1. Summary of dual action approach.*

## REFERENCES

1. Parad HJ (ed): Crisis Intervention: Selected Readings. New York, Family Services Association of America, 1966
2. Koos EL: Class differences in family reactions to crisis. Marriage and Family Living, 12:3, 1950
3. Epperson MM: Families in sudden crisis: Process and intervention in

a critical care center. Social Work in Health Care, Vol. 2 No. 3, Spring 1977
4. Goldsborough JD: On becoming nonjudgemental. American Journal of Nursing, November 1970
5. Garrett A: How to interview. *In* Interviewing, It's Principles and Methods. New York, Family Service Association of America, 1972
6. Bard M, Zacker J: The prevention of family violence. Dilemmas of community intervention. Journal of Marriage and the Family, November 1977

## RECOMMENDED READING

Burgess AW, Lazare A: Victims of violence. *In* Community Mental Health: Target Populations. Englewood Cliffs, NJ; Prentice-Hall, Inc., 1976
Eliot TE: Handling family strains and shocks. *In* Family, Marriage, and Parenthood. Boston, Heath and Co., 1955
Johnson R, Trimble C: The (expletive deleted) shouter. Journal of the American College of Emergency Physicians, Vol. 4, 1975
Jordan L: Teamwork at the accident scene. The Police Chief, September 1976
Kahn R: Conflict, ambiguity, and overload. Three elements in job stress. Occupational Mental Health, 3:1, 1973
Kroes W, Hurrell Jr. J, Margolis B: Job stress in policemen. Journal of Police Science and Administration, 2:2, 1974
Langsley DG, et al: Family crisis therapy, results and complications. Family Process, 7:2, 1968
Lindemann E: Symptomology and management of acute grief. American Journal of Psychiatry, 101:141, 1944
Parad HJ, Caplan G: A framework for study in families in crisis. Social Work Journal, Vol. 5, 1960
Rangeli L: Discussion of the Buffalo Creek Disaster. The course of psychic trauma. American Journal of Psychiatry, 133:3, March 1976
Resnik HLP, Ruben H (eds): Emergency Psychiatric Care: The Management of Mental Health Crisis. Bowie, MD; The Charles Press, 1972
Satir V: Communication: Talking and listening. *In* Peoplemaking. Palo Alto, CA; Science and Behavior, Inc., 1972
Selye H: Distress In Life. New York, McGraw-Hill, 1956
Selye H: Stress Without Distress. New York, J.B. Lippincott Co., 1974
Soreff S: Sudden death in the emergency department: A comprehensive approach for families, emergency medical technicians and emergency department staff. Critical Care Medicine, 7:7, July 1979
Vallman RR, Ganzert LP, Williams WB: The reactions of family systems to sudden and unexpected death. Omega, November 1971

Wachowiak KD: Sudden infant death syndrome: What you can do to help the family. R.N., February 1978

Weinstein S: Sudden infant death syndrome: Impact on families and a direction for change. American Journal of Psychiatry, 135:831, 1978

Wilson JQ: What makes a better policeman. Atlantic Monthly, Vol. 223 No. 3, 1969

CHAPTER **6**

# Childhood Crisis

Ann Scanlon-Schilpp, R.N., M.S.

## INTRODUCTION

Children in crisis present a complex challenge for crisis workers. Children in various age groups have specific needs and respond differently to the same crisis events. In addition, children undergoing severe stress frequently regress or return to behavior below their level of development. Another serious problem encountered by crisis workers is that they have a tendency to become emotionally involved with the children they are attempting to help. Emotional involvement frequently interferes with the proper crisis management.

Among the many events that produce a crisis state in a child or adolescent's life, injury, illness, and death are considered the most disruptive. The emphasis in this chapter will be on the care of children who are faced with these and other serious crises.

This chapter will review the main points of the intellectual, emotional, and social development of children in different age groups. By recognizing these developmental levels in children, crisis workers will be in a better position to develop an intervention plan that will be the most effective in the crisis situation.

Although the basic principles of crisis intervention discussed in Chapter One apply to the child as well as to his family, the special needs of children frequently call for special intervention techniques. The information and techniques suggested in this chapter will be most helpful in assisting emergency service personnel in the proper crisis management of children.

## BACKGROUND

During the first year of life, the major causes of infant death are primarily infections, specifically those of the respiratory and gastro-intestinal tracts. The mortality rate decreases drastically after one year, and the major cause of death in the years leading up to and through adolescence is accidents.[1] The toddler (ages one through three), who now is beginning to explore his environment, is particularly vulnerable to such injuries as burns, falls, vehicular accidents, and ingestion of foreign materials like drugs, cleansing agents, insecticides, and more. The high incidence of death and disability due to accidents in the one to five age group occurs because:

1. The child has little ability to understand cause and effect relationships.
2. The child has little past experience upon which to draw, and use of judgment is not yet a part of his intellectual capabilities.
3. The child imitates adult behavior.
4. The concepts of motion and time are not developed.
5. Muscular coordination is not developed.
6. The child explores his world by bringing it to, and into, his mouth.[2]

The school age child and the adolescent frequently incur injury outside of the home. They are involved in automobile accidents, falls, drownings, or in athletic accidents. Between the ages of five and fifteen, accidents still rank as a leading cause of death. The incidence, however, drops markedly during this period, only to rise again dramatically during late adolescence.[2]

In order to assess the child, it is important to understand the process of growth and development. Since children are in a state of continual change, the job of assessment is a complicated one. Growth essentially refers to an increase in size (weight or height), while development refers to an improvement in skill and functional capacity.[3] This process, though varying to some degree from child to child, is an orderly one. Intellectual growth is markedly influenced by the child's social environment as well as by his emotional experiences. The focus of assessment here will be concerned with the child's psychosocial abilities, specifically his intellectual, emotional, and social development.

## A CHILD'S PSYCHOSOCIAL DEVELOPMENT

| INTELLECTUAL | EMOTIONAL | SOCIAL |
|---|---|---|
| | Birth to Two Years | |
| Reflexive behavior: cries when wet, hungry, frustrated, or in pain. | Learning to trust people and environment: most important person is mother or caretaking figure. | Primary source of socialization is family and this occurs within the home environment. |
| Gradual development of behavior with a purpose. | | |
| Interest in new things. | Needs: response to physical needs by mother through touching. | |
| Unable to form concepts. | | |
| Uses symbols and symbolic play. | | |
| Imagination. | Security, safety. | |
| Distinguishes "me" from "not me." | Poor defenses against anxiety: crying, biting, throwing objects, hitting, head banging, rocking, sucking thumb, carrying "security blanket." | |
| Memory development. | | |
| Can minimally infer causes from observing effects. Can predict effects from observing causes. | | |
| Self-centered. Has difficulty in appreciating other's point of view. | | |

| INTELLECTUAL | EMOTIONAL | SOCIAL |
|---|---|---|
| | Age 2-4 years | |
| Language development. | Learning to be autonomous. | Primary sources of socialization are family and peers: learns through play with others, can cooperate with another child in play. |
| Imagination, "pretends." | | |
| Imaginative behavior: verbal and physical (dresses up like Dad or Mom: repeats things parents have said in his presence). | Moving away from tight attachment to mother: learning independence, dressing self, washing, feeding. | |
| Learning through play. | Situations need to be structured as to kinds of choices. | Learning to share. |
| Intellectual growth occurs by child gathering information through his senses from environment. | | |
| Major sense organs utilized for information processing are: the eyes and mouth. | Needs outside control and limits set on behavior, but given freedom to try and freedom to explore. | |
| Magical thinking: believes because he wishes something, it happens. | | |

| INTELLECTUAL | EMOTIONAL | SOCIAL |
|---|---|---|
| | **Ages 4-7** | |
| Fills gaps in his knowledge through questioning and experimenting "How come," "Why," "What's this."<br><br>Uses all of his senses now in gathering information.<br><br>Ability to make judgments through primitive problem solving.<br><br>Concept formation as child; now has more past experiences to which he can relate present situation. | Learning initiative.<br><br>Seeks immediate gratification of wishes. | Primary source is family and to a small degree peer group.<br><br>Can cooperate with other children in trying to achieve goal in play.<br><br>Sharing. |

| INTELLECTUAL | EMOTIONAL | SOCIAL |
|---|---|---|
| | **Age 7-12** | |
| Communicates about shared topics of interest.<br><br>Sees others' viewpoint and not just his own.<br><br>Concept of time, space, and motion developing.<br><br>Still concerned with the present and needs objects to manipulate to make logical relationships.<br><br>Difficulty in projecting into future.<br><br>Operates on trial and error. | Tolerates limited separation.<br><br>Developing sense of independence.<br><br>Cooperates and understands treatment efforts with simple explanations.<br><br>Has developed some defenses to cope with anxiety (denial, and magical rituals such as crossing fingers). | Family and peer group.<br><br>Spends most of time with groups of children.<br><br>One special friend. |

| INTELLECTUAL | EMOTIONAL | SOCIAL |
|---|---|---|
| Age 12-18 | | |
| Considers possibilities even without experiencing them: not bound to what he can see and touch. | Strives for independence from family: parents target for this conflict. | Peer groups exerts strong pressure. Prone to taking irresponsible risks. |
| Considers hypothesis. | Seeking to find identity to "Who am I," "Where am I going." | |
| Uses logic in deductive and inductive reasoning without having to use observation. | | |
| Understands cause and effect relationships. | Body image is an important issue. | |
| Learning taking place through abstraction. | Need for limit setting. | |

The above material is used with the permission of Blake, Wright, Waechter: *Nursing Care of Children*. New York, J. P. Lippincott Co., 1970

## ASSESSMENT AND INTERVENTION

In assessment of the child, it is important to consider the following: age, past experiences with injury, what the child was doing when the injury occurred and what the child's developmental level is. Past experience plays a significant role in how the child deals with new situations. If he has been well cared for by his parents; if he has had his physical, social, and emotional needs met, then his response to you will be one of trust and respect for your authority. He obviously will be frightened and, possibly, panicky but approachable.

For the child under six, separation from his mother provokes the greatest anxiety. [4] He also fears pain, as well as disapproval. In the immediate treatment of the child in this age group, it is extremely important that the mother or caretaker be present to provide some security. The mother needs to be told what to do and needs help with maintaining her composure. Simple direct statements to the mother need to be given by the crisis worker. "It's okay to touch your child on the head," "hold his hand," "talk to him." Children between six and twelve are usually hurt doing things that their parents have warned them not to do. Often, the child fears retaliation or punishment from the parent. Guidance

65

for the mother needs to include a statement that lets her know that while it is okay to be angry with the child, her support and comfort are what he needs now. [5] Other intervention techniques are as follows:

- Since children are quite aware and sensitive to what is happening around them, as well as what is being said, it is important to monitor the conversation that the child will hear.
- It is also important to prevent him from seeing things that will be upsetting, particularly if a brother, sister, or parent is involved in the accident.
- This applies to children who are bystanders as well.
- These children should be escorted away from the scene of an accident by an adult. They should be given brief, simple information about what is happening.
- When approaching the child who has been hurt, the emergency service worker needs to do so calmly and gently.
- Tell the child your name and who you are.
- If the child is alert enough and can communicate, ask him his name, where he hurts, and what happened to him.
- The child's response to your question will tell you the degree of crisis he is in: if he can tell you where he hurts and some information about what happened, it means that his thinking is clear and an avenue for supporting him is now open to you.
- Just as adults can problem solve and cooperate more effectively when given information, so also can the child and adolescent. Simple, brief explanations of what you are going to be doing should be given prior to touching the child: "I'm going to look at your left arm now, Eddie," or "I'm going to take off your shoe, Eddie," or other explanation.
- Always call the child by his name.
- If something painful has to be done, such as an IV insertion, prepare the child for it. "This will hurt some, Eddie, when I put the needle in your arm. It's okay to cry real loudly."
- When you are finished doing the painful procedure or treatment, tell the child it is over and that he handled it well.

- Trust develops when the child is provided with the truth, as painful as it might be.
- Always tell the child about the painfulness of a treatment *before* it is given.
- If the child is capable of being given a choice, and if the situation allows for that, let him make the choice.
- If the child is physically able to help (for example, hold a bandage for you) let him do that.
- Try to make many procedures for the younger child into games.
- Selection of words when talking to a child is important. Be simple and honest. [2, 5, 6, 7]

A child's behavioral responses to injury can range from screaming and crying, to silence. It is important that the emergency service worker accept the child's behavior and his manner of expressing his fear. For the child who is quiet, ask if he is frightened and what might help him. Give him a suggestion like, "Would you like me to hold your hand?" (A great deal of touching is important when dealing with children.) Tell him it is okay to cry or holler if he wants to.

For the young child (age zero to three), who cannot communicate his needs and fears verbally, simple explanations are still needed. Should the mother be present, she should be allowed to stay with the child enroute to the hospital. Also, the helper needs to ask if the child has a favorite blanket or toy that may be given to the child to hold.

If the crisis worker has developed some rapport with the child, this should continue enroute to the hospital. If not, the individual making the initial contact should then introduce the child to another person who will be taking care of him. If time permits, the child should be told that he is going to the hospital and he should be told what he can expect to happen there. [7]

In situations where both parent and child are hurt, the parent needs information about what is happening to the child, and reassurance that someone is with the child, caring for him. The child also needs the same information about his parent.

## SOME PRECAUTIONS FOR CRISIS WORKERS

1. Do not leave the child alone.

2. Do not threaten the child with punishment if he is uncooperative.
3. Do not tell him things like, "Big boys don't cry," or "You're acting like a baby."
4. Do not lie to child, "This is just a little stick," when in fact it hurts.
5. Do not frighten the child in order to gain cooperation. ("You'll die if this IV is not inserted.")
6. Do not talk about the child's family or living conditions in front of child.
7. Do not criticize the parents in front of the child.

It is generally believed that parents love and protect their children from the horrors of the world, and yet tragedies occur both to children who have supervision as well as to those who do not. The emergency service worker must be aware of:

1. His own responses to the circumstances surrounding the injury and,
2. The needs of the family during this crisis. No matter what the circumstances of the accident may be, it is important to meet the emotional needs of the family first, *and to do so objectively.* It is imperative *not* to make comments like, "If you had been there, this wouldn't have happened to your child," or any statement that reflects the fact that they were not caring appropriately for their child. Deal with the "here and now" and how they can be supportive to their injured child. [2]

One's own feelings need to be discussed with peers after traumatic situations rather than be kept inside of oneself. The crisis worker may have a child of his own and is reminded of this fact by the child with whom he is working. This identification can elicit many different feelings in the individual. These feelings may include anger, fear, or helplessness. If this identification does occur, the crisis worker may become emotionally distressed at the scene and may act disorganized. Removal from the situation by peers is necessary, and follow-up emotional care should be provided for this individual. (See Chapter 15 on stress and burn out.)

## PREVENTION

Emergency service personnel have the potential to act in many roles within the community they serve. Besides their primary work in law enforcement and emergency intervention, crisis workers may also function in a prevention role. The crisis situation which they have been called upon to manage may often have other problems attached to it. Recognition of these problems may prevent future difficulties because they have made an accurate initial assessment of the entire situation. A child who has been injured in the home may be the calling card for the crisis worker's entrance into the situation. Once there, he may recognize another child's need for health care, or a family's need for home-safety education. Referrals concerning these areas can either be offered to the family, or made to the appropriate agency (law enforcement, medical, or social services) at that time.

Rapid intervention by other agencies can prevent many cases of neglect, abuse, or ignorance which might produce maiming and/or death.

## REFERENCES

1. Suchman E, Scherzer A: Current Research in Childhood Accidents. New York, Association for the Aid of Crippled Children, 1960
2. Blake, Wright, Waechter: Nursing Care of Children. New York, J. B. Lippincott Co., 1970
3. Alexander EE, Alderstein AM: Studies in the psychology of death. *In* David HP, Brenghman JC (eds): Perspectives in Personality Research. New York, Springer Publishing Co., 1960
4. Blake, Wright, Waechter: Separation Anxiety: A critical view of the literature. New York, Child Welfare League of America, Inc., 1964
5. Miles M: Body integrity fears in a toddler. Nurs Clin N Am, 4:39, 1969
6. Almy M: Young Children's Thinking. New York, Teachers College Press, 1967
7. Geist H: A Child Goes to the Hospital: The Psychological Aspects of a Child Going to the Hospital. Springfield, IL; Charles C. Thomas, 1965

## RECOMMENDED READING

Appleby M, Trumbull R: Psychological Stress. New York, Appleton, 1967
Blake F: In quest of hope and autonomy. Nurs Forum I:8, 1961

Brown R: Language: The system and its acquisition. *In* Social Psychology. New York, The Free Press, Collier-Macmillan Limited, 1965

Cobb B: Psychological impact of long term illness or death on the family circle. J Pediat, 49:746, 1956

Doland D, Adelburg K: The learning of shared behavior. *In* Child Development, 1967

Erikson EH: Childhood and Society. New York, Norton, 1963

Ervin-Tripp S: Language development. *In* Hoffman M, Hoffman L (eds): Review of Child Development Research Vol. II. New York, Russell Sage Foundation, 1966.

Flavell J: The Developmental Psychology of Jean Piaget. New York, Van Nostrand, 1973

Flavell J: The role of bodily illness in the mental life of children. Psychoanal Stud Child 7:68, 1952

Glass DC (ed): Environmental Influences. New York, The Rockefeller University Press and Russell Sage Foundation, 1968

Grantley W, Bernasconi M: The concept of death in children. J Genet Psychol, 110:71, 1967

Heinicke C, Westheimer I: Brief Separations. New York, International University Press, 1965

Hymovich DP: ABC's of pediatric safety. Am J Nurs, 66:1768, 1966

Katan A: Some thoughts about the role of verbalization in early childhood. Psychoanal Stud Child, 16:184, 1961

Kidd A, Livoire J (eds): Perceptual Development in Children. New York, International University Press, 1966

Kidd A: Early education: A cognitive-developmental view. Child Development, 39:1013, 1968

Lazarus RS: Psychological Stress and the Coping Process. New York, McGraw-Hill, 1966

Lewis MM: Language, Thought and Personality in Infancy and Childhood. New York, Basic Books, 1963

Lindemann E: Symptomatology and management of acute grief. Am J Psychiat, 101:144, 1944

Luschen M: Technique and temperament made the difference. Am J Nurs, 64:103, 1964

Piaget J: The Origins of Intelligence in Children. New York, International University Press, 1965

Robson K, Pedersen F, Moss H: Developmental observations of diadic gazing in relation to the fear of strangers and social approach behavior. Child Development, 1969

Stevenson H (ed): Child Psychology. Chicago, Chicago University Press, 1963

Verwoerdt A: Communication with the Fatally Ill. Springfield, IL; Charles C. Thomas, 1966

Yarrow LJ: Separation from parents during early childhood. Review of Child Development Research Vol. I, New York, Russell Sage Foundation, 1964

Yarrow LJ, Goodwin MS: Effects of change of mother figure during infancy on personality development. Progress report. Washington, DC; Family & Child Services, 1963

# Chapter 7

# The Alcohol Intoxicated Person

Jeffrey T. Mitchell, M.S.

## INTRODUCTION

Alcohol intoxication can complicate any emergency call. It jeopardizes the safe, efficient, and successful handling of most crisis situations. There are over one-hundred million drinkers in the United States today, [1] and alcohol is the most widely used drug of abuse. It is close to impossible for the average public safety worker to avoid all contact with intoxicated people while working in the field.

Recent studies have demonstrated that close to sixty percent of all auto accident fatalities, sixty percent of all murders, forty percent of assaults, forty percent of rapes, sixty percent of suicides, and fifty percent of fire deaths involved alcohol. [2]

Alcohol intoxication is a problem of immense proportions and has no easy solution. It is a problem for emergency service personnel as well as families and employers. Perhaps some of the information and guidelines presented in this chapter will help them deal effectively with this great problem.

## PROBLEM SOURCES IN INTOXICATION

There are two sources of problems in managing the intoxicated person:

- The crisis worker's attitudes
- The intoxicated person

Those who are called upon to intervene with the intoxicated person usually have little training to do so and have even fewer guidelines to deal with the situation. [3,4] The greatest difficulty for emergency personnel is to overcome their own emotional reactions, prejudices, and expectations concerning intoxicated persons. Frequently, past experiences with relatives or bad experiences with other intoxicated people pollute their handling of the

73

current situation. One study recently pointed to the fact that emergency medical technicians treated sixty-seven percent of lacerations correctly if no alcohol abuse was involved. However, only fifty-eight percent of laceration injuries were treated correctly when the patients were intoxicated. [5]

The intoxicated person, himself, is also a major source of problems for the crisis worker attempting to manage an alcohol related crisis. Intoxicated people can be loud, obnoxious, uncoordinated, and uncooperative. Their behavior frequently disrupts attempts to help them.

The best remedy for these problems is for the crisis workers to become aware of their own thoughts and emotions regarding alcohol use and abuse. It also helps to become as well educated as possible about alcohol, its effects, and the plight of the abuser. The next section of this chapter will provide some of the basic information necessary for understanding and managing alcohol crises.

## BACKGROUND MATERIAL FOR ALCOHOL AND ALCOHOLISM

Alcohol is a chemical substance made up of carbon, hydrogen, and oxygen atoms. It is produced by the fermentation or distillation of grain or wood and is produced in three major types—ethyl, denatured, and methyl. [6]

Ethyl alcohol (or grain alcohol) is obtained from the action of yeast on grain or fruits such as corn, oats, grapes, and apples. Ethyl alcohol is fit for human consumption. Denatured alcohol is ethyl alcohol that has been made unfit for human consumption by the addition of toxins. Denatured alcohol is used as a solvent. Methyl alcohol is also unfit for human consumption. It is commonly called "wood alcohol" because it is distilled from wood. Methyl alcohol is a poison, and it frequently produces sudden blindness and death. [6,7]

Ethyl alcohol is rapidly absorbed into the blood stream from the small intestine and it is carried to every cell in the body. [8] Every type of human cell is damaged to some degree by the presence of alcohol. Obviously, the higher the alcohol intake, the higher the level of damage. The body's overall aging process is accelerated by alcohol. [9] Because the brain is the most sensitive organ in the body, it is subject to the most damage. Very high levels of alcohol have been known to demyelinize the cells of the brain. [10] This means that the insulation that keeps brain cells from short circuiting is reduced or eliminated. In addition to its effects on body cells, alcohol complicates every disease already present in the body.

Alcohol is both a stimulant and a depressant. It provides an immediate source of calories to the body at a high level. These calories provide energy and a sense of euphoria. The person consuming alcohol will feel warm, "high," and ready for action. The stimulating effects of the drug are rapidly burned off, however, by the body's metabolism and the depressive (or sedative) effects of the alcohol set in. Also, the blood cells have a tendency to clump (agglutinate) when in contact with alcohol. The clumping prevents the blood cells from entering the tiny blood vessels to keep the surface of the skin warm. A person who is drinking and exposed to cold is more prone to getting frostbitten. [9]

Alcoholism can be defined as a primary, progressively pathological, constitutional reaction (disease) to alcohol ingestion. [1] There are about ten million people in the United States who experience the disease. About fifty percent of all of the people who became alcoholic show symptoms of alcoholism at the very beginning of their drinking experience. There are three major symptoms of alcoholism. They are:

A. An uncontrolled desire to drink, which is usually triggered by a small amount of alcohol.
B. Black out spells.
C. A strong physical dependence which makes withdrawal difficult, dangerous, and sometimes results in death. [1, 6, 11]

Research has led many scientists and health professionals to believe that the alcohol produces a lesion (or scar) on the hypothalamus of the brain. [9, 12] The hypothalamus is partially responsible for the control of many major functions such as the body's endocrine activities, emotions, body temperature, fluid balance, food intake, and the inhibitory mechanisms which help us to control our behavior. [13] Once the hypothalamus is damaged, the person can be considered truly alcoholic. He has almost no control over his drinking once he begins a drinking episode.

It should be carefully noted that alcoholism is not a psychiatric disease. Certainly, psychiatric factors play a big role in the development of the disease in many cases. Any psychiatric problem that is already present in the person is intensified by the presence of alcohol in a person's system. [10, 11] *However, in one-hundred percent of all cases, the primary cause of alcoholism is alcohol and all psychological or social factors play a secondary role!*

## ASSESSMENT

It is *not* the job of public safety personnel to determine whether or not one is an alcoholic. That diagnosis can be made only after a careful evaluation by specially trained personnel within the medical and behavioral science fields. Therefore, the remarks which follow are, in most cases, applicable to people who are either truly alcoholic or who are just experiencing simple intoxication.

## STAGES OF ALCOHOL INTOXICATION

### *Blood Alcohol*

| Number of Drinks | Content | Effect |
|---|---|---|
| 1 highball or equivalent | 0.03% | No noticeable effect |
| 2-4 highballs or equivalent | 0.05% to 0.12% | *Mild high* Varying effects on different people. Effects range from feelings of warmth and relaxation to fine motor uncoordination and moderate unsteadiness in walking. |
| 8 highballs (½ pint whiskey) | 0.15% | *Acute Intoxication* Effects are gross impairment of bodily and mental functions. |
| | .15% and above | Stupor and coma may result. |
| | .55% | Fatal |

76

1. *The Mild High.* Small amounts of alcohol produce a variety of effects in humans. They may feel excited, enthusiastic, or elated. Others may experience mild fatigue, relaxation, warmth, and a feeling of peace. Mild uncoordination of fine muscles, slowed reaction time, and gastro-intestinal disturbance may also be present. No special treatment is necessary and the effects will wear off in about one to three hours. [7, 14, 15]

2. *Acute Alcohol Intoxication.* If a person continues to drink beyond the mild high, he will sooner or later enter the acute intoxication stage. The person in this stage is profoundly uncoordinated, has slurred speech, and may experience swings in behavior which range from feeling very happy to feeling depressed and ready to cry. A person in the acute intoxication stage may be "funny" and make people laugh, but he is also prone to sudden fits of violence. He frequently cannot remember what he has done to others even less than an hour later. Normally, no special medical treatment is required. Once this person "sleeps it off" his behavior will return to normal.

If there is any doubt as to the person's medical well being, he should be brought to a hospital. In cases where there is no danger of medical complications, it is appropriate that the person be brought home and left in the care of his relatives. He should be brought to jail by the police only if he was involved in the commission of a crime and only if no danger of medical problems exist. [14, 15, 16]

3. *Alcohol-Induced Stupor.* The person whose drinking has gone beyond the acute intoxication stage enters a stupor. Police officers and ambulance technicians frequently find this individual in alley ways or lying on the street. He is usually unconscious, but, if conscious, is unable to make sense out of who he is or where he lives. He may just stare blankly and not respond to questions. *Because falls are very common in this group of drinkers, potential head injuries need to be carefully checked.* [15, 16, 17]

4. *Alcohol Coma.* This is a much more serious alcohol produced problem in which the person is completely unconscious, and has no response to the deep pain reflex or other stimuli, such as shouting his name. It is impossible to tell in the field whether coma has been produced by alcohol, a head injury, or a disease like diabetes. Comatose people must be taken to a hospital for evaluation. Poor care of this alcohol emergency can produce

death. Respiratory function, depression, and heightened cardiac problems are common and the person is at risk. [17, 18]

## THE WITHDRAWAL FROM ALCOHOL

Since alcohol is a drug which produces a physical dependence, withdrawal from the substance is dangerous and frequently deadly. Some detoxification centers in the United States have reported death rates as high as thirty percent. [1] People withdrawing from alcohol are usually sick and need help.

The severity of withdrawal symptoms depends on several factors:

1. Duration of intake. The longer the period of time a person has been drinking, the more difficult will be the withdrawal process.
2. The amount of alcohol ingested. Obviously, the higher the amount, the greater the risks.
3. The abruptness of cessation in drinking. Those who stop drinking suddenly usually have more problems than those who reduce their alcohol intake gradually.
4. Individual susceptibility. Each person has a somewhat different capacity to handle alcohol in the body. A small sized teenage girl will be more affected by the same amount of alcohol than will a well built truck driver who has been drinking alcohol for fifteen years. [19]

## STAGES OF WITHDRAWAL

1. *Tremulous stage.* This is the mildest withdrawal. The person may experience any or all of the following: mild tremors of the fine motor muscles, headache, nausea, flushed face, and agitation. This stage can, in some cases, last several days and may progress to more serious symptoms. A good, balanced diet, observation and emotional support are ususaly most helpful. [16, 17, 20]

2. *Acute hallucinosis stage.* The person usually has all the symptoms of tremulous stage, but also experiences visual, auditory or tactile hallucinations (unreal perceptions in the person's

78

mind). Usually, these hallucinations pass in a day or two, but there have been some cases of hallucinations lasting several months! People in the acute hallucinosis stage are best treated in a medical facility or in a special detoxification center.

3. *Delirium Tremens (DT's)*. This most severe stage of withdrawal usually shows up between one and seven days after the last drink. [15] This stage is characterized by tremors, hallucinations, and disorientation in the person (cannot identify himself), place (cannot tell where he is), and time (has lost all concept of time). The person usually has a high fever, is delirious, sweating profusely, and has severe agitation. Tachycardia (rapid heart rate) and convulsions may also be present. This situation is a true medical emergency and hospitalization is certainly indicated. No unconscious person should be left at home or placed in jail. [17, 21]

## OTHER IMPORTANT CAUTIONS ON ALCOHOL ABUSE

A. *Methyl Alcohol Poisoning*. People who ingest methyl alcohol are in a serious risk of death. [14, 17] They obtain the methyl alcohol from sterno, wood alcohol, antifreeze, and hair tonics. They experience sudden impaired vision, central nervous system depression, muscle incoordination, intense abdominal pain, delirium, cyanosis (blue coloring around the finger tips and lips), difficulty in breathing, and a weak, irregular pulse. Their eyes are extremely photosensitive (sensitive to light) so they should be protected from strong light. *Immediate hospital treatment is essential.* [14, 17]

B. *Alcoholics Being Treated With Antabuse (Disulfiram)*. Many alcoholics agree to be treated with a drug to help them control their drinking. The drug is called Antabuse. Crisis workers should be alerted to the fact that any exposure to alcohol can make these people violently ill. Exposure to rubbing alcohol (for IV's) or substances which contain alcohol for cleaning hands after fingerprinting is dangerous. They will experience flushing, sweating, difficulty in breathing, chest pain, headache, and a severe drop in blood pressure which might produce death. Drowsiness, nausea, and vomiting are also present at times. [18, 22, 23]

C. *Alcohol and the Psychotic Person*. It should be noted by crisis workers that even a small amount of alcohol will produce serious emotional problems in a person who is already prone toward mental disturbance. [1, 11]

D. *Alcohol and Suicide.* People who drink alcohol are more prone to carry out suicidal threats. Alcoholics commit suicide at a rate that is fifty-eight times higher than the general population. [24]

E. *Alcohol and Other Drugs.* Almost all drugs react differently when alcohol is present in the body. Alcohol and another central nervous system depressant may combine in the system and produce an extremely strong reaction. It may even cause death. [25]

## INTERVENTION WITH THE ALCOHOL INTOXICATED PERSON

### Assessment and Intervention

Both a physical and emotional assessment is essential if the crisis worker is to be safe, and the intoxicated subject is to be cared for properly. Assessment is done in the following order: *look first, then talk,* and *finally take action.*

Here are some general guidelines and suggestions for a successful assessment and crisis intervention.

### Assessment

1. Look first. Get a clear picture of the scene and the people involved. (Note your escape routes also.) Get a first impression in your mind by gathering as much visual information as you can.
2. Unless the person is unconscious, do not touch him until you establish some working relationship. *Talk and listen before touching.*
3. If it is nighttime, do not shine your flashlight directly in the person's face. This will antagonize him.
4. Avoid working alone if at all possible.
5. Introduce yourself. Tell the person that you are there to help.
6. Ask questions carefully and do not rush. If you get resistance from the person on a question, skip it. Return to the question later if necessary.

7. Talk to the person with respect. Address him by name. Keep accusing tones out of your voice. Do not laugh at a person or ridicule him.

8. Do not argue with an intoxicated person. You just will not win.

9. Find out if alcohol is causing the current crisis. When did the person have his last drink? What was he drinking (beer, wine, vodka, or some combination)? Has he ever had DT's or convulsions after drinking?*

10. * Ask about allergies and whether or not other drugs have been mixed with alcohol. On Antabuse?

11. * Ask about whether the person has any diseases such as diabetes, peptic ulcer, heart problems, or others.

12. Ask the person's permission to touch him before moving him. You may say something like this, "It looks to me like you hit your head. Can I take a look at you? I'll try not to hurt you." or "Can I bandage that hand for you? It looks like it's bleeding quite a bit."

13. Perform as complete a physical assessment as possible. Do a full body survey and make sure you get the vital signs such as blood pressure, pulse, and respiratory rate. Note bruises and bumps. An intoxicated person's blood does not clot as well, and a person can easily bleed to death internally if he has been injured. Do not forget the medical history.

14. Keep the person's airway open, especially if he is unconscious.

* Note: *If a yes answer is obtained for the starred items, hospitalization is indicated.*

## Intervention Techniques

1. Avoid loud noises and abrupt movements. They can frighten a disoriented person and cause him to become violent.

2. It is okay to offer the alcohol intoxicated person a cigarette, candy, water, or fruit juice (if this is not in opposition to local policies). No alcoholic beverage should be offered because it may precipitate a more intense problem later.

3. Before transporting an intoxicated subject, a brief explanation of where he is being taken and what is going to be done should be made. "We're going to take you to a hospital so a doctor can make sure you didn't hurt yourself."

4. Never lie to an alcohol intoxicated person.

5. The intoxicated subject should not be placed in a brightly lit room (his eyes are sensitive to light). Also, he should not be placed in a room with shadows. (Shadows increase the frequency and intensity of visual hallucinations for the intoxicated person.)

6. Keep the person in touch with reality. Neither agree or disagree with hallucinations. "I don't see the snakes, but you might see them."

## Violent Persons in Alcohol Crisis

1. If a person appears violent or if violence becomes imminent, avoid touching him. Above all else, protect yourself and keep your escape routes open. Do not try to deal with such a person alone.

2. Try to talk the person down. If it looks like that is not going to work, and violence is about to break out, retreat, get plenty of help, and try again if necessary. You have some distinct advantages over an uncoordinated, confused person.

3. If absolutely necessary, restraints, which do not cut off circulation or cut into the skin, may be used. Most of the time they are not necessary and usually make a situation worse.

4. Make sure the hospital emergency department is notified that an intoxicated person is being brought in.

5. If a relative or friend is having a calming and controlling influence on the intoxicated person, he may be allowed to accompany the person to the hospital or police station.

6. Whenever possible crisis workers should be in civilian clothing. They should also remove pins, badges, pens, pencils, and other sharp or loose objects from their pockets.

7. A calm, firm, confident, and professional attitude will do

much to assure the smooth handling of an intoxicated person.

8. Avoid IV techniques if possible. (But local medical protocol should be followed.)

9. Keep crowds away from the person. They usually urge a person to show off or get violent.

10. Special police tactical squads exist in many communities for disarming people who are threatening violence with a weapon. Do not hesitate to call upon these highly trained teams if the situation is serious or threatening.

11. The intoxicated person should not be left unattended, as occasionally happens in *some* jails across the country. The proper place for many intoxicated people is in a hospital facility if there is any danger of injury or illness.

12. The unconscious person should be turned to one side so should he vomit, vomitus will not be sucked (aspirated) into his lungs.

13. Treat respiratory or cardiac problems as necessary.

14. Take suicidal or homicidal threats seriously.

Note: The above guidelines were taken from many sources. See especially references 4, 7, 11, 14, 15, 16, 17, 18, 20, 21.

## REFERENCES

1. Milam R: The Emergent Comprehensive Concept of Alcoholism. Kirkland, Washington; Alcoholism Center Associates, Inc., 1974
2. De Lissovoy G: From a lecture on "Alcoholism" during a behavioral emergencies workshop. Charleston, WV; H.E.W. Emergency Medical Services Conference, Impact 79, October 1979
3. Metropolitan Washington Council of Governments, Emergency Medical Services Council: Criteria for the Care of the Behavioral Emergency. Washington, DC; C.O.G. EMS Council, 1977
4. US Department of Transportation, National Highway Traffic Safety Administration: Management of the Emotionally Disturbed. *In* National Training Course, Emergency Medical Technician Paramedic: Instructor's Lesson Plans Module—XIII. Washington, DC; US Government Printing Office, 1977
5. Frayier W, Cannon J: Emergency Medical Technician Performance

Evaluation. *In* NCHSR Research Report Series. Washington, DC: National Center for Health Services Research May 1978

6. Thomas L: Alcohol. *In* Taber's Cyclopedic Medical Dictionary, 12th ed. Philadelphia, F.A. Davis Company, 1973

7. Ottenberg J, Rosen A, Fox V: Acute Alcoholic Emergencies. *In* Resnik HLP, Ruben HL, (eds): Emergency Psychiatric Care: The Management of Mental Health Crisis. Bowie, MD; The Charles Press Publishers, Inc., 1975

8. Scarans J: Emergency Response: The Alcohol-Intoxicated Patient. *In* Emergency Medical Services. September/October 1979

9. Alcohol, The Inside Story. A supplement to Listen Magazine, Vol. 25, No. 10, Washington, DC; Narcotics Education, Inc., 1973

10. Rees ULL: A Short Textbook of Psychiatry. Philadelphia, J. B. Lippincott Company, 1976

11. Kolb C: Alcoholic Psychosis and Alcoholism. *In* Modern Clinical Psychiatry. Philadelphia, W. B. Saunders Company, 1977

12. Knisely H: Brain Damage Starts with the First Drink. Listen, Vol. 22, No. 12, 1970

13. Gardner E: Fundamentals of Neurology. Philadelphia, W. B. Saunders Company, 1975

14. Grant H, Murray R: Emergency Care, 2nd ed. Bowie, MD, Robert J. Brady Co., 1978

15. The Committee on Allied Health, American Academy of Orthopaedic Surgeons: Emergency Care and Transportation of the Sick and Injured, 2nd ed. Menasha, Wisconsin; George Banta Co., Inc., 1977

16. Anderson RH, Weisman M: The Alcoholic in the Emergency Room. Maryland State Medical Journal, July 1969

17. Hathaway S: Primary Care in Alcoholism. *In* Crisis Intervention and Psychiatric Emergencies Workbook. Baltimore, Maryland Institute for Emergency Medical Services, 1975

18. Gazzaniga AB, Iseri LT, and Baren M: Emergency Care: Principles and Practices for the EMT-Paramedic. Reston, VA; Reston Publishing Co., Inc., 1979

19. American Automobile Association: You . . . Alcohol and Driving. Falls Church, VA; American Automobile Association, 1975

20. Knott DH, Beard JD, Fink RD: Alcoholism, The Physician's Role in Diagnosis and Treatment. *In* Twenty-Fourth Annual Scientific Assembly of the American Academy of Family Physicians, September 1972.

21. The International Association of Chiefs of Police: The Effects of Alcohol. *In* Training Key # 18. Gaithersburg, MD; 1964

22. Weisman N: The Use of Disulfiram in the Treatment of Alcoholism. Maryland State Medical Journal, March 1968

23. University of Maryland: Antabuse, facts for the family. Baltimore, Alcoholism and Drug Abuse Program, 1976

24. National Council on Alcoholism: Facts on Alcoholism. New York, National Council on Alcoholism, Inc., 1973

25. Greenblatt DJ, Shader RI: Drug Interactions in Psychopharmacology. *In* Shader RI (ed): Manual of Psychiatric Therapeutics. Boston, Little, Brown and Co., 1975

CHAPTER **8**

# Substance Abuse

Jeffrey T. Mitchell, M.S.

## INTRODUCTION

The management of crises by emergency service personnel is difficult under normal circumstances. Add *substance abuse (any deliberate, excessive, and persistent use of a substance which alters a person's physiological or psychological status)* to a crisis, and the complexity of management can come close to overwhelming the resources of those who wish to help.

Substance abuse requires a high degree of sensitivity among the crisis workers. It entails an array of medical, legal, and behavioral complications that are rarely found in other types of crisis. Some drugs can produce dangerous or deadly reactions in the user. Disease symptoms may be masked or exaggerated by the drugs. Substance abuse is a criminal activity and emergency service personnel, particularly the police, must be aware of the illicit nature of the abuse. Likewise, they should be careful in maintaining the crime scene as well as in the handling of evidence. In addition, some drugs produce bizarre, violent, or frightening behavior.

This chapter is written to provide a set of useful guidelines for emergency service personnel who must cope with a substance abuse crisis under field conditions. Except where it was necessary to enhance the understanding of the drug reactions to achieve proper management in the field, the medical and legal aspects of the individual substances have been de-emphasized. Instead, the behavioral aspects and the correct techniques for the crisis care of the abuser have been emphasized.

## BACKGROUND

It is easy to speculate that drug abuse is as old as drugs themselves. Man has persistently sought out substances to alleviate anxiety, elevate a mood, and to provide pleasure. Alcohol and herbs have been used throughout recorded history. [1]

Drug abuse is present when the substance is used outside the bounds of acceptable medical or social practice. Most of the substances which are abused act upon the central nervous system in a manner that affects mood, feelings, or behavior. [1]

With extended use of many drugs, a drug dependence may evolve. A *drug dependence* is a compulsive desire to continue using the drug either to further the pleasurable aspects of the drug or to avoid the discomfort of withdrawal. Drug dependence may be either physical or psychological.

*Physical dependence* is an altered physiological state which is produced in the body by repeated exposure to the substance. This means there are changes in the body chemistry, and withdrawal from the substance brings about a set of specific symptoms.

A *psychological dependence* is the emotional motivation behind the drug use. The user believes that the drug is necessary to maintain his sense of well being. He is, therefore, unwilling to curtail his drive to use the drug. [1,2]

There are six general classifications of substances that are abused. The last five are addressed and regulated by Title II of the comprehensive Drug Abuse Prevention and Control Act of 1970 (Controlled Substances Act). [3] The six classifications of substance abuse are:

1. Volatile Substances
2. Cannabis
3. Narcotics
4. Depressants
5. Stimulants
6. Hallucinogens

The type of physiological and psychological reactions to substance abuse depends on a number of factors. Changes in the following factors may produce changes in the reactions a person has to the drug he is abusing:

A. *Type of drug.* The chemical structure and dosage is important.

B. *Physical Characteristics.* The size, weight, and metabolism of a person may make some difference in the drug reaction.

C. *The Situation.* Where the drug is administered, whether the person is alone or with a friend, the emotional atmosphere and the way the person is treated, all have negative or positive effects on the user.

D. *The Set.* The set is considered to be the attitudes, the expectancies, and the motivation of the user.

E. *The Personality.* A person's previous psychological state, current personality characteristics, and prior drug experience may combine with the drug to cause unexpected reactions.

F. *Tolerance.* Tolerance means that a person must gradually increase the amount of the drug necessary to achieve the same effects. A term closely associated with tolerance is cross-tolerance. This means that a person who is tolerant to one drug may be tolerant to similar drugs within that drug classification, even without prior exposure to them.

G. *Presence of Contaminants or Other Drugs Concurrently (poly drug use). Drugs mixed together may produce some dangerous or highly unusual reactions and may even be death-producing.* [2, 4, 5, 6]

As in dealing with alcohol emergencies, the emergency service worker has two major difficulties in dealing with other forms of substance abuse. One of those difficulties stems from within the crisis workers themselves. It consists of the attitudes, experiences, expectations, and prejudices which come into play during the crisis and prevent the proper management of the substance abuser. The other source of difficulty can be found within the personalities of the abusers. The major factor here is that a mixture of drugs and unknown personalities can produce highly unpredictable results.

Of the two, the most serious difficulty is the one which comes from within the crisis worker. More than any other factor, negative attitudes, anger, and displaced hostility by the crisis worker will increase the dangers and difficulties inherent in intervention with a substance abuser.

## ASSESSMENT AND INTERVENTION

When dealing with substance abuse cases it is difficult to know what to do unless you have a good idea of what kind of substance has been abused. Various substances produce different reactions in the body and mind. Some knowledge of the main classifications of abused drugs and their typical reactions can be helpful to emergency service personnel.

The emergency service worker needs to know some basic information to make an evaluation of the substance abuse situation. The type of substance, its amount or dosage, the manner in which it was taken, and how recently it was taken will be the most helpful information. These facts must be combined with observations regarding the user's level of consciousness, behavior, and overall medical condition. Emergency service personnel will usually be treating a person symptomatically. That is, they attempt to treat the presenting problem even if the symptoms deviate from the textbook norm. For example, if a drug abuser is suspected of using a stimulant, but shows symptoms of respiratory distress, he is treated for the respiratory distress first and the other problems later.[7]

Since this book is concerned with emergency interventions in crisis situations, it would be inappropriate to list every kind of abused drug with the many symptoms which may occur for each. Instead, brief presentations for each of the six major substance abuse classifications will be given along with a description of the more common reactions. Also, those classifications demanding the fewest crisis intervention techniques will be discussed first. This will allow for a more extensive coverage of the classifications of substances which require crisis intervention.

## VOLATILE SUBSTANCES

- Paint
- Solvents
- Aerosol Propellants
- Gasoline
- Nail Polish
- Thinner
- Kerosene
- Model Glue
- Lighter Fluid

These substances are usually inhaled through the nose and mouth. The abuser experiences light headedness, tingling sensations, and intoxication similar to alcohol intoxication. Rashes around the nose, identifying odors, containers, and other paraphernalia are the best indicators of this kind of substance abuse.

Exposure to volatile substances produces perceptual motor disorientation, slurred speech, and mucous membrane irritation in the nasal passages. In higher doses, central nervous system

88

depression, anemia, brain damage, kidney and liver damage, coma, and death may result. [8]

## TREATMENT OF VOLATILE SUBSTANCE ABUSE

- Remove the person from the fumes.
- Provide oxygen.
- Observe vital signs (pulse, respiration especially).
- Be prepared to resuscitate.
- Provide emotional support with crisis intervention techniques.
- Transport to a medical facility for physical and emotional evaluation.

| CANNABIS | Examples of Common Street Names: |
|---|---|
| Marijuana | Pot |
| Tetrahydrocannabinol (THC) | Grass |
| Hashish | Maryjane |
| Hashish oil | Weed |

Cannabis (marijuana), one of the most frequently abused drugs, is being researched as a medical drug for the control of nausea and vomiting in patients being treated with chemotherapy for cancer, and for reducing pressure in the eyes of people suffering from glaucoma. Outside of those two instances, there are no other current medical uses of the drug. [9]

Depending on the experience and expectations of the user, marijuana may produce restlessness, a sense of well-being, relaxation, increased appetite, changes in thoughts and sensory perception, and reddened eyes. High doses may produce image distortions, fatigue, feelings of paranoia, loss of personal identity, fantasies, and hallucinations. Excessive doses may produce a toxic psychosis.[9]

It would be inaccurate to state that use of marijuana is harmless. Many scientists have demonstrated its harmful effects. (Refer especially to references 10, 11, 12, 13, and 14 for further information.) Besides, it is not the purpose of this chapter to argue the benefits or deficits of marijuana. What needs to be said, however, is that uncomplicated use of marijuana (that is, cases where no other drugs are involved) usually does not present a medical or emotional problem to emergency services workers. There may be occasional outbursts of violence or an occasional episode of psychosis in an emotionally disturbed patient who has used marijuana. The management of the typical patient calls for no special medical or crisis intervention techniques. The establishment of a good working rapport, the use of communication skills, and a referral to the hospital or (when necessary) to law enforcement agencies is the treatment of choice in most cases. (It is assumed that emergency personnel are called upon because there is a medical problem; or the user is creating a disturbance or because he has been involved in an accident.)

| NARCOTICS | Examples of Common Street Names: |
|---|---|
| Opium | H |
| Morphine | Horse |
| Codeine | Junk |
| Dilaudid | Smack |
| Heroin | Brown sugar |
| Demerol | Morf |
| Methadone | Mud cube |
| LAAM (Levo Alpha Acetymethadol) | |
| Darvon | |
| Talwin | |

With the exception of heroin, which has no current medical use, narcotics are usually used to reduce pain and induce sleep. Narcotics are highly addictive both physically and psychologically. Although they are generally injected, they may be taken orally, sniffed, or smoked. The usual effects are euphoria, drowsiness, slowed respiration, constricted pupils, and sometimes nausea. An overdose may kill because it depresses the respiratory system. Convulsions and coma are frequent with narcotic overdose.

Withdrawal from the drug is a painful process characterized by watery eyes, runny nose, loss of appetite, tremors, panic, chills, cramps, and excessive sweating. [15]

## INTERVENTION TECHNIQUES

- There is a serious risk of respiratory arrest in the narcotic abuser. The emergency personnel must be prepared to resuscitate should breathing cease.
- Narcan (naloxone HCl) may be given to counteract respiratory depression. This, of course, may only be given after a physician's order to a certified paramedic or a nurse. This drug has a short half life, so be prepared for repeated administrations.[16]
- Pinpoint pupils may indicate other problems, so do not overemphasize their presence or lack of them.
- Do not waste too much time looking for needle tracks on the arms. Most narcotic abusers have found more interesting places on the body in which to inject themselves. (The nail beds and the penis are not uncommon spots for injection.)
- Transport to the hospital.
- Few other specific crisis intervention techniques are useful here. Most abusers are very drowsy or asleep during their treatment.
- The potential for violence is higher in the narcotic abuser during the withdrawal stage.

| DEPRESSANTS | Examples of Common Street Names: |
| --- | --- |
| Chloral Hydrate | Downers |
| Barbiturates | Red devils |
| Doriden | Yellow jackets |
| Quaalude | Rainbows |
| Equanil | Blue heavens |
| Dalmane | |
| Valium | |
| Librium | |
| Serax | |
| Miltown | |

Depressants act upon the central nervous system as sedatives, hypnotics, and pain killers. The user most frequently experiences fatigue, slurred speech, disorientation, drunken behavior, lowered anxiety, and sleep. Overdoses, or the combina-

91

tion with alcohol or another depressant, can be deadly. An overdose usually produces depressed respiration, systemic shock,
and coma.

Withdrawal from long term abuse of central nervous system
depressants is extremely dangerous and should *not* be attempted outside of a hospital. Anxiety, tremors, delirium, convulsions, and death may result.[17]

## INTERVENTION TECHNIQUES

- Induce vomiting if less than thirty minutes has passed
  from the time of ingestion.
- Transportation to a medical facility is a must.
- No specific crisis intervention techniques are utilized in
  most cases since the abuser is usually extremely drowsy
  or asleep.

| STIMULANTS | Examples of Common Street Names: |
|---|---|
| Cocaine | Uppers |
| Amphetamines | Crystal |
| Preludin | Dexies |
| Ritalin | Bennies |
| | Jellybeans |
| | Meth |
| | Pep pills |
| | Speed |

Stimulants are used medically as local anesthetics, for
hyperactivity in children, and in weight control. Abusers are at-
tracted to stimulants because they produce an increased sense of
alertness and excitement. In addition, there is a sense of
euphoria, increased heart rate and blood pressure, and a loss of
appetite. Overdosing may produce agitation, hallucinations,
convulsions, and death. Stimulants are capable of producing a
strong psychological dependence and may be physically addicting.[1,18]

Since the crisis intervention treatment of both stimulants
and hallucinogens are practically identical, specific intervention
techniques will be listed after the section on hallucinogens
which follows.

## HALLUCINOGENS

LSD
Mescaline
Amphetamine Var-
    iants (STP,
    DOM, PMA)
Phencyclidine
    (PCP)
Psilocybin

## Examples of Common Street Names:

Acid
Flakes
Mushroom
Magic mushroom
Angel dust
Hog
Peace pill
Sunshine
Windowpane

With the exception of phencyclidine (PCP) which is occasionally used as an animal tranquilizer, the hallucinogens have no current medical uses. They are not considered physically addicting, but have a moderate potential for psychological dependence. They work directly on the mind and produce illusions and hallucinations, as well as poor time and distance perception. High levels may produce "bad trips" which are longer, more intense periods of illusions and hallucinations. Psychotic reactions and death are not uncommon. PCP is particularly troublesome since it is totally unpredictable and may cause extreme violence.

## CRISIS INTERVENTION IN BAD TRIPS

The guidelines presented here are most useful if emergency service workers are faced with drug reactions and "bad trips" in abusers of stimulants and hallucinogens.

## GENERAL PRINCIPLES

- Treat medically according to symptoms.
- Protect self, patients, and others if necessary.
- Monitor vital signs.
- Be confident and in control.
- Reassure the user.
- Be alert for changes.

- Preserve crime scene (Be alert for drug paraphernalia such as blotter paper, wrappers, chemical equipment, glycine bags, pill bottles, syringes, and other material).
- Transport to a medical facility.
- Reduce the anxiety and calm the person.
- Focus on the here and now.
- Limit the intervention goals to what is accomplishable in the current problem.
- Be aware of your limitations and do not go beyond them.
- Avoid using street names of drugs unless you are very familiar with them. They change too fast and the wrong name will hurt the building of rapport with a user. [20]

## Specific Techniques

- Do not argue.
- Do not agree or disagree with abuser's distortion of reality.
- Use friends of the victim to help you calm him down.
- Allow the person to speak freely and to express himself.
- Keep them in contact with reality.
- Do not interrupt.
- Take your time.
- Provide a quiet, uninterrupted room.
- Touch victim gently if he or she allows it.
- Let them move around but confine them to one room.
- Only one emergency service worker does the talking. This should be the person who has the best rapport with the victim and who seems to understand the crisis most.
- Keep the person warm.
- Give food, juice, or other nutrition.
- Do not work alone.
- Do not make quick movements.
- Cut down on stimuli.
- Do not give any further medications.
- Do not leave victim alone.

## THE TALK DOWN

Do your talking in a soft, calm, even tone. Tell the person that the strange things he is experiencing are caused by the drugs and that he is not going crazy. Tell the victim that the bad experiences will soon pass. Let him know repeatedly that he is safe and will not be harmed. Communicate in factual, non-judgmental, and realistic manners. Provide support, care, empathy, and warmth.

Most importantly, suggest to the person that he imagine that he is in a very pleasant, quiet place and that he is not in any danger. Tell him to imagine that he is with very friendly people and is surrounded by beautiful flowers with pleasant colors and smells. (Or ask him what would be pleasant for him at this time and suggest that he imagine only the pleasant things.) If the person becomes frightened during the talk down, provide more reassurance and suggest more pleasant things. Do not allow him to stay with frightening thoughts. Suggest safety, peace, quiet, and anything pleasant that you can imagine. When the experience becomes more pleasant and the person becomes quiet, you may gently lead him to the ambulance for transport to the hospital. Keep suggesting pleasant experiences on the way to the hospital.

- Shut off flashing lights before bringing victim out of the house.
- Cut down bright lights inside ambulance.
- Do not use the siren, unless you have a true medical emergency.
- Obtain a consultation with the hospital if necessary.
- Avoid restraints unless it becomes absolutely necessary. (Once they are applied they should be kept in place.)[21]

## CLOSURE

Once you arrive at the hospital, it will be necessary to turn the care of the substance abuser over to hospital personnel. The abuser will be frightened and will need assurance that these people will continue to care for him and will not allow him to be harmed. The crisis worker may have to spend a few extra minutes making sure that the transition is smooth. Hospital personnel should be informed of the victim's condition at the scene so they might be ready for that type of behavior should it reoccur in the emergency room.

Finally, referrals for continued care should be made by public safety or hospital personnel. The referral may be accepted more readily by the abuser who is in a state of crisis because he may realize his own resources are limited. The crisis may be one of the few times in his life that he understands how much he needs outside help to resolve his drug problem.

## REFERENCES

1. Levine RR: The Pharmacological Aspects of Drug Abuse and Drug Dependence. *In* Pharmacology: Drug Actions and Reactions. Boston; Little, Brown and Company, 1978
2. Shader RI, Caine ED, Meyer RE: Treatment of Dependence on Barbiturates and Sedative-Hypnotics.*In* Shader RI: Manual of Psychiatric Therapeutics, Practical Psychiatry and Psychopharmacology. Boston; Little, Brown and Company, 1975
3. Drug Enforcement Administration: The Controlled Substances Act. *In* Heath H(ed): Drug Enforcement. Washington, DC; US Government Printing Office, 1979
4. Barber TX: LSD, Mescaline, Psilocybin, and other Psychedelic Drugs. *In* LSD, Marijuana, Yoga, and Hypnosis. Chicago, Aldine Publishing Company, 1970
5. Greenblatt D, Shader RI: Bad Trips.*In* Shader RI: Manual of Psychiatric Therapeutics, Practical Psychiatry and Psychopharmacology. Boston; Little, Brown and Company, 1975
6. Drug Enforcement Administration: Clandestine Laboratories. *In* Heath H(ed): Drug Enforcement. Washington, DC; Government Printing Office, 1979
7. Gazzaniga A, Iseri LT, Baren M: Emergency Treatment of Poisoning. *In* Emergency Care: Principles and Practices for the EMT-Paramedic. Reston, VA; Reston Publishing Company, Inc., 1979
8. Grant H, Murray R: Medical Emergencies: Alcohol and Drug Abuse. *In* Emergency Care, 2nd Ed. Bowie, MD; Robert J. Brady Company, 1978
9. Drug Enforcement Administration: Cannabis.*In* Heath H(ed): Drug Enforcement, Washington, DC; Government Printing Office, 1979
10. Hollister LE: Human Pharmacology of Marihuana (Cannabis). *In* Harris RT, McIsaac WM, Schuster CR (eds): Drug Dependence. Austin, Texas; University of Texas Press, 1970
11. Leuchtenberger C, Leuchtenberger R: Cytological and Cytochemical Studies of the Effects of Fresh Marihuana Cigarette Smoke on Growth and DNA Metabolism of Animal and Human Lung Cultures. *In* Braude MC, Szara S (eds): Pharmacology of Marihuana, Vol. 2. New York, Raven Press, 1976

12. Maugh II, TH: Marihuana (II): Does it Damage the Brain? Science Vol. 185, August, 1974
13. Jones HB: What the Practicing Physician Should Know About Marijuana. Private Practice, January 1976
14. Robbins PR: Marijuana: A Short Course. Boston, Braden Press, Inc., 1976
15. Kuehnle JC: Drug Abuse Problems and Their Management. *In* Bernstein JG (ed): Clinical Psychopharmacology. Littleton, MA; PSG Publishing Company, Inc., 1978
16. Endo Laboratories, Inc: A Comparison of the Narcotic Antagonists Used in Anesthesiology Today. New York, Endo Laboratories, Inc., May 1975
17. Slaby AE, Lieb J, Tancredi LR: Handbook of Psychiatric Emergencies. New York, Medical Examination Publishing Company, Inc., 1975
18. Drug Enforcement Administration: Stimulants. *In* Heath H (ed): Drug Enforcement. Washington, DC; US Government Printing Office, 1979
19. US Department of Transportation: Basic Training Course/ Emergency Medical Technician, Instructor's Lesson Plans, 2nd Ed. Washington, DC; US Dept. of Trans., 1977
20. Leukefeld CG: Behavioral Crisis Intervention and Drug Abuse. *In* Cowley RA: Collected Papers in Emergency Medical Services and Traumatology. Baltimore, Maryland Institute for Emergency Medical Services, 1979 (originally presented at EMS Symposium, 1976)
21. Mitchell JT: Drug Abuse and Crisis Intervention. Paper presented at the Seminar on the Prevention of Alcoholism and Drug Dependency, University of Maine, July 13, 1976

# CHAPTER 9

# Violence in Field Situations

Lawrence D. Messier, M.A.,
Denis J. Madden, Ph.D.,
Jeffrey T. Mitchell, M.S.

## INTRODUCTION

Intervention with a violent individual will be a demanding test of the crisis worker's ability to remain calm and think clearly. Situations prone to violent behavior include family and civil disturbances, alcohol and drug ingestions, and the gathering of large crowds such as at mass spectator events. According to many social scientists, violence is increasing and is a major problem in today's society. In this chapter, we will briefly explore the reasons for violent and aggressive behavior and the methods for productive intervention.

## BACKGROUND

Violence or aggressive behavior may be defined as simply an attack or hostile action directed against a person or thing. This also includes violence directed at one's self such as suicide (see Chapter 12).[1]

Most violent incidents involve normal people who experience a temporary loss of control over their behavior. Males between the ages of 15 and 30 are involved in violent behavior more than any other group.[2] The potential to behave violently exists in every individual. Three essential characteristics of violent behavior which should be remembered are:

1. Violence is a defensive reaction.
2. Violence produces more violence.
3. Violent episodes are time limited.

Many factors have been cited as contributing to violent behavior. Social disorganization, poverty, discrimination, and child rearing practices are commonly associated with higher rates of violence. Research suggests that there are four major causes of violent behavior. These are presented to aid the crisis worker in his attempts to intervene in such cases. A thorough knowledge of these causes is critical to successful intervention.

1. *Physical Causes.* Brain disease or dysfunction may directly cause violent behavior. The violence may be accompanied by memory loss, impaired vision, epileptic seizures, and feelings of panic. For such individuals, an act of violence is usually not an isolated event, but one in a long history of violent incidents. The person may also have a history of traffic accidents and violations or sexual assaults. Their violent behavior may be explosive and can be triggered by even small amounts of alcohol. Even if there is a direct relationship to organic problems, it does not rule out psychological factors such as frustration and threat. [3]

2. *Frustration.* Violent behavior may be aroused by thwarting and frustrating experiences. The sequence occurs in the following order:

FRUSTRATION → RAGE → AGGRESSION

If the individual is constantly blocked from meeting some success (Frustration), → he experiences a feeling of intense anger (Rage), → which is then expressed in his behavior as violence directed toward the source of frustration (Aggression). The aggression has as its goal the removal of the object of frustration and a clearing of the path to the desired goal. Sources of frustration may be failure to win at sports, being denied promotion, or unfair treatment by others. Most people experience such frustration as part of everyday life but are able to control their feelings of anger. The violence-prone individual, on the other hand, has a low tolerance for frustration and desires immediate gratification of his needs. [4,5]

3. *Threat.* As previously mentioned, violent behavior is a defensive reaction. Anticipation of harm of any kind will likely evoke a violent response. The threat may be physical such as suffocation, beating, or other injury. The threat may also be psychological in nature. Embarrassment,

ridicule, rejection, or other threats to one's self image are psychological threats. The threat may be real or imagined. When a person reacts violently he usually perceives the threat as real and imminent. It should also be noted that an aggressive response to one object or individual may be transferred to other objects or people. A person may, for example, not be able to target his feelings against a specific person such as his spouse or his employer so he may turn his anger toward a rescuer even though he is not really angry at the rescuer. [5,6]

4. *Alcohol and Drugs.* Violent behavior is usually an impulsive response. Alcohol and many drugs have the effect of diminishing a person's self control. In most people, it will reduce self control to the degree that violence may occur although there is no previous history of violent behavior. In addition, violent behavior is a common part of withdrawal from addictive substances. Use of these substances must be seen as a potential stimulus for violent behavior. [3,7]

## ASSESSMENT OF THE VIOLENT PERSON

Violent episodes are not too difficult to assess. In many cases the violence will have taken place prior to the arrival of the emergency service personnel. Comments by the victim or bystanders or obvious injuries and destroyed property will be the best indicators.

In some situations, violence may be ongoing when emergency personnel arrive on the scene. Little assessment is necessary in this circumstance and the immediate task is a calm, controlled intervention designed to reduce the amount of stimuli and tension. Protection of self, others, and the violent person is the priority.

In situations in which violence has not yet occurred, assessment is essential. If the crisis worker is not aware of the potential for violence, he may be caught off guard by a violent outburst from the victim. Another danger is that the unsuspecting crisis worker can easily trigger a violent outburst by his statements or actions.

101

There are a number of signs which may signal potential violence. Agitation and threatening statements or gestures are the primary signs. Others are:

- Clenched fists.
- Gritting of teeth.
- Pounding of fists on a table or other objects.
- Loud, sharp speech.
- Obvious muscle tension in the face, hands, and limbs.
- A high level of activity such as rapid walking, wringing of hands, or frequent shifting of position.
- Inability to cope with stress.
- Impulsiveness.
- Paranoid statements.
- Headache.
- Dizziness (Present in a small number of cases.) [8,9,10]

*The very best predictor of potential violence is a history of previous violence.* It is likely that if a person committed violent acts in the past, he is prone to use violence to deal with his current problems. Wife beating, child abuse, and a history of arrests for assault indicate an increased likelihood of violence in the present situation.

An adequate assessment of potential violence can be obtained only by talking directly to the person involved. Potentially violent people frequently express fears of acting in a violent manner, or they may speak of violent or homicidal thoughts toward others. In some cases, they may even discuss actual plans to hurt others. Emergency service personnel should view this type of discussion as a request for help. The violent person actually wants help so he does not hurt someone.[6]

If alcohol or drugs are present in a person who has a history of violence, the dangers of a violent outburst are substantially increased. In fact, emergency service personnel would be wise to exert extra caution because the situation may be explosive.

Physical size should not be looked upon as an indicator for or against violence. Even a small sized person can exert enormous physical force although such situations are quite rare. A large person is not necessarily more violent than a smaller person.

102

## INTERVENTION SKILLS

The first action when arriving at the scene of an ongoing violent activity is to cautiously separate the disputants using a tone of voice that is calm, and with as little force as necessary. If only one individual is the focus of attention, he should be separated from the crowd. Do not spend time trying to find out what is happening from the bystanders. The violent person may begin to believe that you are working with them and he will not cooperate with you. Instead, get him aside alone and talk directly to him. Ask him why all these people seem to be making a fuss about him.

Remember, the violent person feels out of control and is usually terrified of his own uncontrolled feelings. His violence is his last defense against feeling totally helpless. Most violent people actually welcome the restoration of control by a calm, concerned helper. So, treat the violent individual as a person and be confident in your own ability to help. In spite of your own justifiable fears, enter the situation with as much calm as you can.

Be aware of your own prejudices and expectations. If you are not, they may pop up when you least expect them to and you could jeopardize the entire situation.

Do not be upset by your own fears. Anyone who is not fearful of a violent or potentially violent person is quite foolish and living dangerously. Sometimes, the easiest way to manage your own fears is to state them clearly to fellow workers. In most circumstances, it does not hurt to let the violent person know you are frightened (but not panicked). For example, a crisis worker might say, "Hey, what you are doing is pretty scary stuff." This often gives that person a sense of some control in the situation and he may calm down a little.

It takes time to deal with violence. Do not rush right in and attempt to settle the situation instantly. Move slowly, except when a life or someone's well-being is in danger.

It is usually better if emergency service personnel do not try to disarm a person immediately. Remember, time is a major factor in lessening violent potential. If you wait a little, the violent person may be more prone to put the weapon down on his own. This is especially so if you have been able to calm his fears and restore some control. Taking a weapon from someone is always more dangerous than if he voluntarily puts it down. Other factors to keep in mind when intervening are:

- Delay is the name of the game in managing violence. Calm,

103

continuous talking helps to delay. Offering food, cigarettes, and non-alcoholic drinks also helps.

- Utilize good listening skills (see Chapter 2). Use good eye contact; face the person and listen intently.
- Leave the door to the room open and allow the person to have access to the door (without, of course, cutting off your own escape route). This helps an agitated person feel less trapped. If you fear that the person will flee and therefore endanger others, place extra manpower outside the doorway.
- Only one person should talk to the violent person *without interruption* from outside.
- Avoid being punitive and judgmental, and be careful not to take sides.
- Focus on the here and now problem.
- Explore solutions to the problem with the person.
- Help them find "face-saving" alternatives to the violence.
- Do not touch a violent person. They usually react to touching as a threat or as a sexual advance. Also, keep your distance from the person.
- Try to engage their cooperation. You might say, in as non-threatening a way as possible, "If you work with me, things will go more smoothly. I want to help you. I'd like to work with you. If we work together, we can bring some order to this situation. We can handle things better if we work together. I'm not here to fight with you. I'm here to work with you and help you."
- If violence seems to be escalating, protect yourself and others first. Have extra manpower available but do not use it immediately. Sometimes just showing that you have available force will make a person thinking of violence back down. Have an adequate show of force (about four people is usually sufficient). An overwhelming show of force might cause a person to panic.
- Do not draw a weapon unless there is a clear threat to life. Showing a weapon may also cause panic.
- If you must take a person by force, do so quickly using only that force which is necessary. The object is to restore control, not combat the person. Violence on the part of crisis workers usually only brings more violence from the victims.

- Use padded restraints or at least wide bands of leather or cloth. You do not want to hurt, you simply want to control. Handcuffs are not usually a good idea on a tossing, kicking, biting person as they tend to cut into the skin. Once restraints have been placed properly, they should not be removed until the person is in the care of medical personnel and is calm and acting normally. Even when restraints are in use, the crisis worker should talk to the violent person in a calm manner. Psychological calming is used simultaneously with the proper restraints. If a person is placed in a seclusion room, it is necessary that he be carefully observed. The suicidal risk is very high in a violent situation.

## HOSTAGE SITUATIONS

Incidents involving hostages are particularly dangerous. The lives of innocent people are frequently in danger. It would be impossible to provide adequate coverage of such incidents here so a few, simple guidelines will be offered. It should be noted that the taking of hostages for political purposes is a sensitive matter to be handled by highly trained state and federal officials. No attempt should be made to resolve these situations by oneself.

If a hostage situation should develop, it is best handled by:

- Backing out.
- Delaying.
- Calling in tactical police teams and other back-up personnel.
- Calling in specialists trained to manage such situations.

This might include some mental health professionals. (Intervention skills were obtained from these references: 2,6,9,10)

## CONCLUSION

Additional useful information can be found in Chapter 12 (Suicide), Chapter Two (Communications Skills), and Chapters Seven and Eight (Alcohol and Substance Abuse).

Intervention skills cannot be well developed by simply reading about them. It would be best if emergency service personnel set up drills to practice the skills discussed in this chapter and previous ones. It would be ideal for crisis personnel to be restrained or treated as a crisis victim so they have some concept of how the victim feels.

Note: For training purposes the following audiovisual aids are suggested:

1. "The Prevention and Management of Disturbed Behavior." Videotape. Ministry of Health, Ontario, Canada, 1977
2. "One Step Ahead." Film, 20 minutes. Motorola Teleprograms, Inc. 4825 N. Scott St., Shiller Park, Ill. 60176, 1975

## REFERENCES

1. Chaplin J: Dictionary of Psychology. New York, Dell Publishing Company, 1975
2. West L: The violent patient: Causes and management. Practical Psychiatry, Vol. II, No. 3, April/May 1974
3. Mark VH, Ervin FR: Violence and the Brain. Hagerstown, Maryland; Harper and Row, 1970
4. Kolb LC: Modern Clinical Psychiatry, 7th ed. Philadelphia, W. B. Saunders, 1968
5. Lazarus RS: Patterns of Adjustment and Human Effectiveness. New York, McGraw-Hill, 1969
6. Lion JR: Evaluation and Management of the Violent Patient. Springfield, Illinois; Charles C. Thomas Publisher, 1972
7. Rees, WLL: A Short Textbook of Psychiatry. Philadelphia, Lippincott, 1976
8. Lion JR and Penna M: Concepts of impulsivity: A clinical note. Diseases of the Nervous System, Vol. 36 No. 11, November 1975
9. Lion JR, Bach-Y-Rita G, Ervin FR: Violent Patients in the Emergency Room. American Journal of Psychiatry, 125:12, 1708-1711, June 1969
10. Stegne LR, Croker W: The Prevention and Management of Disturbed Behavior. Ontario, Ministry of Health, 1976

CHAPTER **10**

# The Management of Sexual Assault Victims

Jeffrey T. Mitchell, M.S.

## INTRODUCTION

Unless emergency service personnel have been specially trained to deal with sexual assault cases, they are usually quite uncomfortable in attempting to assist the victims of this violent crime. Some faulty cultural attitudes have been ingrained into most of us. Many myths have grown up around the issue of rape. Personal sexual concerns and taboos are common among people, and crisis workers are no exception. Myths, personal concerns, and taboos make it very difficult for some crisis workers to discuss the sexual aspects of the crime with the victims during crisis interviews, treatment, and investigations.

Reports of rape are increasing rapidly in the United States. This fact alone implies that more and more patrol officers, and other crisis workers will be cast into helping roles for which they have little training and experience.

The focus of this chapter will be to fill in the training gap that presently exists in the area of sexual assault. The police officer as the crisis worker is the focal point, since it is the police officer, more than not, who is the first, and frequently the most important, professional to work with the sexual assault victim. Other crisis workers will find it helpful to read through the section written for the police officers. It contains many useful guidelines which can be easily adapted for use by most crisis workers.

## BACKGROUND

The first major concept that crisis workers need to implant firmly in their minds is that rape is not a crime of sex, but a crime of violence. Rape is one of the cruelest crimes committed by one person against another. It leaves in its wake an unmeasurable level of psychological and physical pain for the victims and their families.[1]

Aggression, humiliation, control, and the infliction of physical as well as emotional pain are the primary motivations for the rapist. The sexual organs serve only as weapons for hurting another human being.[2,3,4] If the crisis workers can switch the focus from the sexual aspects of the crime to its assaultive and aggressive aspects, it is likely that they will be able to function comfortably and professionally when called upon to assist the victim of sexual assault.

Rape is essentially sexual contact without a person's consent. It is usually obtained by a force or threat of force and other forms of coercion.[5] (Some states have recently revised rape laws so that victims do not have to prove force by their physical injuries alone.) This definition of rape applies to both sexes and includes anal, oral, and vaginal sexual contact.[2,3,5] Statutory rape (sexual intercourse with a minor) usually falls under a separate category because there is consent involved on the victim's part.[6] Laws vary from state to state, and crisis workers would be wise to familiarize themselves with the laws in their own states.

Rape is considered one of the fastest growing crimes in the United States. FBI statistics indicate that 56,090 rapes were reported in the United States in 1975. It is estimated that eighty percent of all rapes went unreported.[7] Today, there may be as many as 220,000 rapes a year.[1] In spite of increases in reporting rates, only about forty percent of these rapes are actually reported. Sexual assaults of children number between 200,000 and 500,000 cases.[7] The statistics are staggering, but not as staggering as the trail of physical and psychological devastation left by the assailants.[8]

The stab wounds, bone fractures, human bites, jagged lacerations, and blunt injuries are easy to see and count because they are on the surface. It is much harder to see what is going on inside the victim of a sexual assault. The psychological response to the sexual assault has two components—an immediate and a long term reaction to the crisis. Both reactions are emotionally destructive.

## EMOTIONAL REACTION TO RAPE

Psychologically, the initial or shock phase of the rape crisis victim

108

reaction contains the elements of either active high anxiety or withdrawal and silence. There are also feelings of denial, anger, and nausea. Victims frequently experience sleep disturbances, loss of appetite, gastro-intestinal disturbance, irritability, and the mental suppression of painful memories. One characteristic emotional reaction is that of fear. Most sexual assault victims feel that they have lost their security and are anxious about that loss.[2,3,5]

After a period of time, usually several weeks, the short term reactions give way to deeper, more-difficult-to-assess reactions, which are also difficult to resolve. Fear, although less intense, seems to continue. New feelings of guilt and self blame, however, may enter the psychological picture. Phobias (irrational fears) such as fears of the out-of-doors or excessive fears of being alone or of passing by the crime scene may occur. Nightmares increase in intensity and frequency, and long periods of depression may follow. In some cases, where the victim had preexisting psychological problems, symptoms are aggravated by the attack and brought back to the surface. The long term reactions to rape usually take close to a year to resolve and may take longer, especially if a suspect is prosecuted because the victim must go through the court experience. [3]

During the long term phase of the rape crisis reaction, many victims find it necessary to change their lifestyles since they can no longer cope with life as they knew it before the assault. Too much has been disturbed and they feel a need to change. Problems of adjustment are increased in cases in which the victim knew the assailant. Many change jobs, move into new residences, and move to other states. It is not infrequent that the stresses produced by a sexual assault increase pressure within a marriage to the breaking point.[3,5]

## THE VICTIMS

There is no profile of the typical rape victim. The crime of sexual assault is no respector of age, size, sex, religion, color, geographic location, or economic status. (Most victims are women although men are not exempt. For the purposes of this chapter, the victims discussed will be women. However, men who are raped have similar psychological reactions and crisis workers can draw the necessary parallels.) Any woman is a potential rape victim regardless of whether she is dressed as a prostitute or as a nun.[9]

Sexual assault victims are generally between the ages of eleven and twenty-five. However, there are documented cases of rape victims ranging in age from fifteen months to age eighty-six. None of them "asked" to be assaulted. All suffer deep emotional, and sometimes physical, pain as a result of the assault. These are the only characteristics sexual assault victims have in common. [2,8,9]

## THE RAPISTS

It is a bit easier to establish a profile of a rapist. Even so, it is very difficult to pick one out of a crowd. They are not distinguished by special marks, jobs, states of life, or other obviously identifiable traits. What is known abouut them is that about fifty percent of rapists are married and sexually active within the marriage. Only three percent of convicted rapists are diagnosed as psychotic. [9] Almost all rapists show a greater tendency to express violence openly. They usually feel a very strong need to dominate and control a woman. Many can only achieve an erection when they are exhibiting violence and dominance over a woman. [3,9].

Almost all rapists think of the woman as an object and not as a person during the rape. They are frequently quite surprised to see what the victim looks like during the trial. Most plan their attacks and almost fifty percent of them knew their victims before the attack. In many cases they were related to the victims. The rapists only used alcohol to give them courage or lower their inhibitions in about one-third of the rapes. About forty percent of the time a rapist works with at least one other rapist in a "gang" rape. [9,10]

## LEGAL ASPECTS OF SEXUAL ASSAULT

There is no requirement in most areas of the nation that crimes of sexual assault be reported. [7] This has the advantage of protecting the privacy of the victim, but there is an inherent problem in that protection of privacy. Because reporting of sexual assault is not a requirement, police departments are not able to gather accurate statistics on the number of rapes which occur, nor are they able to increase substantially the number of arrests made for sexual assault. [2] It is a difficult problem with no easy solution.

Because we are dealing with a crisis situation that is also criminal, there is a requirement that crime scenes be preserved until thoroughly investigated. Evidence must be collected and a constant chain of custody of physical evidence must be maintained. Most states still require a fairly extensive evidence package to successfully prosecute a rape case. As it stands now, only about forty percent of the cases have sufficient evidence to bring a suspect to trial.[2]

Therefore, emergency service personnel have an added burden of protecting and maintaining evidence in addition to providing emotional support and understanding to the victim of a crisis.[2]

Emergency service workers should be well aware of the fact that no victim (eighteen or older in most states) is required to take treatment. If it is her informed decision that she does not require medical or psychological attention, no one may force her to have it.

## CONFIDENTIALITY

All crisis situations demand a high degree of confidentiality. The sexual assault crisis demands even more because of the sensitive nature of the problem and the fact that society often victimizes the victim of a sexual assault even further. The incident, and especially the names and personal information of the victim and her family, should not be discussed by crisis workers except in line with official duties. At no time should names, addresses, or other personal data be disclosed to the news media without the informed consent of the victim. Fortunately, many informed newspapers and radio and television stations are becoming more sensitive to the plight of the rape victim and are voluntarily eliminating personal information about the victim from their stories. The information is confidential even from the clergy and rape crisis centers unless the victim agrees to its disclosure.

## SPECIAL NOTATIONS AND CAUTIONS

Rape is one of the most serious of violent crimes. The investigation of this crime requires a staff that is highly trained, skilled, and experienced in the art of investigation. In addition, personnel must demonstrate great stability of character and a tactful, understanding and intelligent approach to victims.

The investigation of rape cases is most closely aligned with

111

homicide. Police departments would be well advised to administratively place rape investigation under the homicide section if they do not have an adequate number of rapes (two hundred or more a year) to establish a separate sexual assault investigation unit. Vice and morals sections must deal with a vastly different set of problems and rape investigations should not be arbitrarily lumped together with them. Remember that rape is a crime of violence, not of passion.[2]

Female police officers should not be assigned to sexual assault investigation teams just because they are women. They should instead have a desire to work on such a team and be able to demonstrate the necessary competence.

Just because an officer happens to be a woman does not mean she will be competent to interview rape victims. Likewise, there is no hard evidence that a male is less capable than a female when handling sexual assault cases. The most important ingredient in successful treatment and investigation is not one's gender, but the sensitivity and experience that the person brings to the task. [2,8]

Rape does not always produce the same emotional reactions in its victims. You cannot separate the experience from the person. If a person reacts to most crises with hysteria, or is paralyzed with fear, she will be prone to react in a similar manner when faced with the aftermath of a rape crisis. If a person is usually calm or silent in the face of other crises, she will, in all probability, handle the new crisis situation (rape) in a similar fashion. [8]

There is no hard and fast rule as to when a victim should fight her assailant and when she should submit. There is a hot controversy over this issue and no one seems to have any of the answers. Many times, if a victim fights back, her attacker will run. In other situations, the attacker becomes even more aroused and increases his violence so the victim's life or physical well-being may be jeopardized. What seems to be certain is that, if the victim reacts to her attacker instantly, she has a chance of escape from the completion of the attack. Reacting means to scream, run, act in a bizarre manner, fight, claw, kick, spit, and a variety of other responses depending on the personality of the victim. Any hesitation substantially increases the probability that the attack will go to completion. Most researchers and writers in the field of sexual assault suggest that a woman should submit when it becomes apparent that her resistance is drawing more violence from her attacker and her life is being endangered by her continued resistance. [2,3,6]

Since rape is a crime of violence in which the attacker uses his sexual organ as a weapon, and since the crime entails the violation of one's anatomy and person, a victim will have the same feelings of terror, violation, and loss of control regardless of whether the contact is anal, oral, or coital. The orifices of the body symbolize the means by which something or someone enters another's personal space. Sexual assault is a forceful intrusion into the life of another, regardless of how it is achieved, and the victim reacts with intense, internal emotion in all cases. Her initial reactions should be accepted with the premise that they are normal. She should be considered normal unless there is a clear history (such as psychosis or retardation) to indicate otherwise. [2,3,6,8]

Many stories circulate through police, fire-rescue and emergency medical agencies that sexual assault victims in general are making up the whole rape story to get revenge on a man or to cover up for their own loose morals. These stories are clearly unfounded. Only ten percent of all rape charges are declared false after investigation. This is no higher than the percentage of false charges for any other crime of violence. Charges of rape by victims should be accepted as true unless intense investigation or court action nullifies them. When the complaint is first made, it should always be considered true. [9]

## ASSESSMENT OF THE SEXUAL ASSAULT INCIDENT AND THE VICTIM

Unless you are dealing with a child, initial assessment in cases of rape is not as complex as some other forms of crisis. Much of what needs to be known is on the surface and not hidden as it is in the assessment of a psychotic or violent person.

*The first task* of a crisis worker is to determine if the victim is still in any physical or life threatening danger. (The assailant may not have escaped and may be present and holding the victim hostage. The victim may have sustained injuries which require immediate emergency medical care.) *The next task* is to determine the emotional status of the victim. Is the victim panicky, out of control, and unable to assist in the assessment of her condition? Or is she reasonably well under control, rational, and able to assist the crisis worker on her own behalf? Is she crying, shaking, tense, restless, withdrawn, silent, smiling, or nervously laughing? (This happens with a number of victims and usually indicates an attempt on their part to cope with the stress of the assault. Inappropriate emotional expressions usually indicate a failure of more appropriate coping mechanisms, thus a higher degree of emotional distress.) [11]

*The third task* of the crisis worker is to determine the extent and limits of the crime scene and the evidence within it or on the victim. A decision must be made on how the evidence is to be preserved to assure a case if prosecution of a suspect is pursued. [2]

## SEXUAL ASSAULT CRISIS INTERVENTION TECHNIQUES

Crisis intervention in all situations begins as soon as the cry for help is heard. In many cases, the dispatcher is the first to hear the call. The special nature of a sexual assault case, with its extremely high potential for serious physical and emotional harm, requires that the call for assistance from a victim receive even more supportive care from a dispatcher than is normally afforded to other types of calls.

The following guidelines are especially helpful for dispatch personnel, but are not exclusive to them.

1. Be calm and supportive. Many rape victims are so terrorized by the experience that they can hardly do more than dial the number for help and state that they have been raped.
2. Listen very carefully. You may only get one chance to hear the location if a distraught victim hangs up too fast.
3. Encourage the victim to speak loudly and clearly.
4. Ask for a description of the suspect, the approximate time of when the incident took place, and the escape route of the suspect. Broadcast this information to responding units.
5. Urge the victim to stay on the line. Frequently, victims become most distressed right after they finish making the call for help.[10]
6. Tell the victim what is being done to help her. "We are sending a patrol car and an ambulance right now. Please *do not* hang up. Try to keep talking to me. They will be with you in a few minutes."
7. Advise the victim not to do anything to destroy the evidence. An emotionally distressed woman is usually not

concerned with evidence preservation so it is often easier to tell her not to do anything at all except talk to you until the police arrive.

8. If it is necessary to clear the line, advise the victim to call a friend or relative and talk to them until the police and or ambulance arrive. Be sure to have a call-back number.

9. Do not discuss any details of the incident with the victim. If the victim blurts out a lot of emotional feeling try to reassure and calm her. If she is giving you more detail than is necessary do not bluntly cut her off. Gently state something to this effect, "I understand how distressing this is to you. An officer will be with you shortly to help you and to take a detailed report. What I need to know now is whether or not this man had a weapon (or some other pertinent question)."

10. Allow the victim to cry. If she is crying, the dispatcher must take a more active role in the call and continue to talk to the victim in a calm, controlled, and gentle manner.[2]

## THE AMBULANCE TECHNICIAN

1. Begin by believing that the victim was raped. Determining the truth or falsehood of her charge is a matter for the police and courts, not EMS personnel.

2. Stay calm.

3. Ask the victim directly, "Are you injured?" Talking directly to her and not to bystanders, relatives, or friends helps her to establish some degree of control over her current life situation.

4. Introduce yourself and state your title or position.

5. Visually survey the victim.

6. *Avoid touching her*. She just went through a horrifying experience with a man and generally speaking, being touched just after the rape, even by other women, is detrimental unless it is done as part of good medical treatment.

7. If there are injuries that need attention, ask her if you might proceed to care for them. (She will expect you to care for her injuries, but asking permission sets up good rapport and helps the victim to feel more in control.)

8. Tell her what you are going to do and why *before* you do it.

9. If there is a need for immediate transportation to a hospital because of the severity of her injuries, make the transport. If her injuries are not severe, it may be appropriate to wait for the police before transporting. This is a judgment situation that depends on the circumstances in each case and established medical protocol.

10. Do not cleanse the wounds unless absolutely necessary. This obviously goes contrary to routine patient care, but the ambulance technicians must remember that foreign bodies in and around wounds may be the evidence that can convict a suspect should the case go to prosecution.

11. Advise the victim not to bathe, douche, urinate, or defecate until after she is evaluated medically and evidence is collected. Drinking and eating should also be discouraged.

12. Do not undress the victim.

13. Do not examine the genital area. Just pad the area with a large bulky dressing if there is an obvious injury.

14. Obtain the best description possible of the suspect and transmit that information plus his last known direction to the dispatcher so that he might relay the information to the police.

15. Ask the victim what she needs most at that time. Most victims ask for police, medical attention, psychological attention, security, or control needs (support of friends) in that order. Some are unsure of what they need. Try to fulfill her needs by calling the police, treating her wounds, getting a friend, or other request. [3,5]

16. Do not leave the victim alone, even momentarily, once you have initiated treatment.

17. Talk to the victim, and keep talking to her. She is a hurt human being. Do not just chatter about irrelevant or trite things like the latest baseball game. Talk to her about pertinent things. "Are you hurt anywhere else?", This bandage isn't too tight, is it?", "Do you feel nauseous?", "Here, it looks like you can use a tissue or two.", "We'll be taking you to the hospital shortly.", "Is there someone you would like us to call?" These are just a few examples of the types of things that can easily be said to

a rape crisis victim.

18. Do not joke. Violence is too serious for jokes.

19. Do not ask her about the rape incident. You may say something like, "I'm sure that was a horrible thing he put you through, but it's over now and you are safe." But do not interrogate or ask for any details. *Do not* ask questions like this, "Why were you here alone so late at night?" (That implies that she is somehow responsible for the attack.)

20. Allow her to cry or express her feelings, but do not probe. Be calm and reassuring, but do not give any false assurances.

21. Say "You're safe now" *not* "Don't worry, he won't ever come back."

22. Keep the crime scene secure.

23. Make the victim as comfortable as possible. Provide pillows, blankets, emesis basin, and other materials as she requests. Try to anticipate her needs (be sure not to damage any evidence if possible).

24. Do not offer her your hand to hold. It could be viewed as a threat. If she takes your hand, without you offering it, that is okay.

25. Keep the victim private. Remove any aggravating people from her presence.

26. Record factual information about the victim's physical and emotional condition on the ambulance record. Do not write, "She was anxious." State instead, "She was stuttering, biting her nails, wandering about aimlessly, and shifting her position. She also was crying softly."

27. Tell her what is going to happen next to the best of your knowledge.

28. Transport the victim to a hospital that has been designated as a treatment center for sexual assault. Most states have specific hospitals that have been designated as sexual assault treatment centers because they have special facilities and equipment for a rape evaluation (evidence kits and written protocols).

29. Once you arrive at the hospital, do not announce in a crowded area that you have brought in a "rape" victim. This will make many people in the waiting room stare at the victim which heightens her discomfort. Just state

that the victim was assaulted. Then quietly tell the nurse or physician that this is a sexual assault case.

30. Above all else, treat the victim of a sexual assault as a consumer of emergency medical services. Treat her with respect and dignity. She is not "dirty" or "unusual," and she needs your support.

## THE POLICE PATROL OFFICER'S RESPONSE TO SEXUAL ASSAULT

1. Respond to the call quickly but without jeopardizing personal or civilian safety.
2. Quickly assess the need for medical treatment, apprehension of the suspects, support units (helicopter, canine unit, crime lab, tactical squad, and others), sexual assault investigation team, and supervisory personnel.
3. Provide for immediate needs (first aid, pursuit and arrest of suspect, reassurance, calls for supervisor and support units).
4. Briefly interview victim regarding time, suspect, description, direction of escape, and other information.
5. Update the "look out" bulletin and have it broadcast by the dispatcher.
6. Reduce the level of activity around the victim. Remove the victim to a private area as soon as possible. This will help to calm her and it insures further cooperation later in the investigation.
7. Assure the victim that she is safe now and you are there to protect her.
8. Preserve the crime scene and evidence. Advise the victim not to douche, bathe, change clothes, eat or drink, and explain why briefly.
9. If you are not designated to perform the in-depth, formal interview, do not ask her any details about the incident. Leave that to the investigators.
10. Allow the victim to express her feelings.
11. Do not touch the victim except to provide first aid or whatever assistance may be necessary (for instance, if she were getting into a patrol car).
12. Make the victim as comfortable as possible.

13. Talk to the victim as much as police duties allow you to, but do not joke or discuss irrelevant things. Tell her what is happening and why.

14. Ask the victim if there is a relative or friend she would want brought to the scene. This helps to establish a support system for her.

15. Have her transported to the hospital if her injuries dictate a need for immediate hospital care.

16. Do not offer false assurance like, "Don't worry, rapists never return to their victims." That is not true! In many cases, the victim was raped a second or third time by the same assailant. Instead, tell her she is safe now. Assure her that she did the right thing in handling herself during the crisis, and the proof of this is that she is alive. Many victims can be spared self doubt if they can be told this early.

17. Utilize arriving support units as dictated by local police policy.

18. Record only factual information on reports. Opinions are out of place.

19. When interviewing bystanders or neighbors as potential witnesses do not state that a rape has occurred. Simply state that a serious crime has been committed and that you are interested in knowing if anyone saw or heard anything unusual.

## COMMAND FUNCTIONS IN SEXUAL ASSAULT

If supervisory personnel have been called to the scene the following guidelines may be helpful in the assistance of the victim and the conduct of the investigation.

1. Set up the command post away from the victim's house. A park, a school building, or a parking lot can be utilized. This serves several functions. First, it keeps unnecessary attention away from the victim's house. Secondly, it helps to avoid interference with crime lab and other functions which may be going on in the house. Thirdly, it assures that the suspect, if apprehended, will not be able to gain any further information about the victim's house, and she will not have to go through the trauma of having the sus-

pect brought back into her house where the crime took place (about fifty percent of all rapes take place in the victim's place of residence). [9]

2. The command post coordinates the search for the suspect.

3. Coordination of witness gathering is also a command post function.

4. Activities of support services are coordinated at the command post.

5. Crowd and traffic control coordination is also a function.

6. The command post has to assure inter-agency communication and cooperation.

7. The command post may call in rape crisis center personnel, friends, relatives, or chaplains, but, only with the consent of the victim. She may not want the help of specific people. So be sure to keep her involved in her own helping process by asking her whose help she wants. [12]

## THE INTERVIEW

1. The formal, in-depth interview should, in most cases, be performed as early as possible. People who are emotionally traumatized, as sexual assault victims are, tend to follow a natural psychological defense mechanism called repression or the "forgetting" of painful material. [11,13]

2. The sexual assault victim's story should be told in great detail only once. Investigators must be very careful not to make the victim psychologically relive the terror of the incident by numerous unnecessary repetitions of her story at the scene.

3. The formal, in-depth interview must always be done in private. The hospital, the command post, a neighbor's house are good spots. If it is not possible to perform the interview anywhere else but the victim's house, it is necessary to hold the interview in a room other than the one in which she was attacked. Sometimes the victim will state a preference for having the interview in her home, and this request should be honored.

4. The victim should be made as comfortable as possible for the interview.

5. Tape recordings may be made, but only with the victim's permission. If a tape recorder is used, it is best to use the smallest one possible so that it can be placed nearby without drawing undue attention. A ninety-minute tape is best because it avoids the interruption of tape changing. The working parts should be covered from the victim's view so that the victim is not distracted. Investigators will generally find that tape recorders can be clumsy devices that can detract from a good interview.

6. Notes on pertinent portions of the story should be made even if a tape recorder is used.

7. The victim should be allowed to go through her entire story without interruption. Once she finishes, the investigator may go back and ask questions and have the victim expand sketchy portions of her story until enough information is given.

8. Good interviews have the four parts mentioned in the chapter on communication skills and interviewing. They are:

   - Introduction
   - Transition
   - Process
   - Closure

9. During questioning, be careful to avoid comments which place the blame and responsibility on the victim.

10. The victim has a right to refuse to make a report. If she does, after the officer or investigator advises her of the advantages and disadvantages of that decision, she should be given a card with the name, unit or section, address, and phone number of an investigator should she change her mind.

11. In the somewhat rare false charge case, the officer or investigator should be aware that people who make false charges are usually emotionally disturbed and are giving a cry for help. It is always more helpful if the interviewer's anger is kept under control and the woman is referred to a counseling center, a woman's group, or to psychiatric services so she can get her problems resolved.

## IDENTIFICATION OF A SUSPECT BY A VICTIM

1. An on-the-scene or near-the-scene identification is appropriate if an apprehension of a suspect has been made. Avoid having the suspect taken to the victim's home. The command post is better. You may also take the victim to the place where the suspect was apprehended or is being held in custody.

2. Do not surprise the victim by suddenly presenting the suspect.

3. Prepare the rape victim to view the suspect by telling her that you would like her help in determining whether or not a certain person was involved in the crime. Do not indicate that you believe the suspect in custody is the perpetrator. The victims of sexual assault are sometimes highly suggestible and may make a positive identification just to please police officers.

4. A victim's emotional distress may prevent her from describing or identifying the suspect. A number of women undergoing extreme stress actually close their eyes for relatively long periods of time in the psychological defensive attempt to keep the experience outside of themselves.

## THE GATHERING OF EVIDENCE IN SEXUAL ASSAULT CASES

1. The following are common bits of evidence in sexual assault cases:

   - Fingerprints
   - Stains on clothing, sheets, carpets, and elsewhere
   - Fibers
   - Hair (scalp and pubic)
   - Clothing
   - Bedding
   - Weapons
   - Broken objects
   - Buttons
   - Fingernail scrapings
   - Pieces of torn clothing
   - Chips of paint
   - Physical injuries
   - Semen
   - Other

2. If articles of clothing or other fibrous material contain blood stains, do not place these items in pastic bags or plastic containers. The plastic enhances the growth and action of bacteria. Bacteria can interfere with the efforts of

122

laboratory technicians to properly type the blood and suspect indentification is rendered more difficult. Paper bags would be better for this type of evidence. [7]

3. Photographs of the crime scene, pieces of evidence, and of the victim should be taken by police. Photographs of the victim's injuries require her consent. The best place to take the photographs of the victim's injuries is at the hospital. Police or medical photographers may do the job. The victim and photographer should sign, date, and write the place where they were taken on the back of the photographs.

4. The presence of semen on the woman's clothing can often be determined by using an ultra violet light. Semen will appear florescent when exposed to an ultra violet light source.

5. Physicians, in addition to examining the victim's whole body, should thoroughly examine and collect specimens from the victim's mouth, anus, and vagina. The results of the physical examination should be carefully documented, and specimens should be analyzed according to the protocol established by local policies. [14]

6. It is essential to maintain a constant chain of custody of all evidence.

7. All procedures should be carefully, and gently, explained to the victim before they are performed to assure that she is not surprised or unduly frightened by police or hospital procedures.

8. Document all evidence with great care. [15]

## THE CLOSURE OF THE TREATMENT, TRANSPORT, AND INVESTIGATION OF THE VICTIM

1. Make sure that the victim's final needs such as transportation home, clothing, or temporary housing are handled before the officers or investigators leave the victim.

2. A draft of a transcript of her formal statement should be made so she can read it. A list of questions should be prepared to fill in any gaps in her original statement. Once all of the pertinent information is on the statement, the victim should be asked to sign the final version according to local law and policies.

3. If it is necessary to show mug shots, the choices should be

123

narrowed to the fewest possible. The confused victim of sexual assault will have difficulty picking a single suspect out of hundreds of photos.

4. Keep the victim informed of new leads in the case and any new developments such as the suspect's release on bail. Continued contact helps the victim to feel that she has not been abandoned by the police.

5. If possible, assist the rape victim in finding continued help. Not all rape victims need professional assistance, but police departments should be able to help a sexual assault victim locate follow-up help in the community.

## CHILD VICTIMS

Molestation and the rape of young children is a particularly disturbing crime inflicted on youngsters (below age sixteen in most cases) by very sick adults. Many of the suggestions for handling adolescent and adult rape situations presented in this chapter will be quite useful and are applicable to child molestation and rape.

There are some specific statements which should be made, however. It is important to avoid any implication of guilt regarding the child. The less focus placed on the child about the incident, the better. Young children (2-7 years old) do not have well formed attitudes and notions about sex. They may view the incident in the same way that they would were they to have been hit over the head by a stranger or if someone had taken one of their toys. Older children (7-16 years old) are psychologically disturbed by the incident and usually need more intensive follow up. They are frequently excessively concerned with pregnancy and bodily well-being as a result of the incident. Do not make the child feel guilty.

Frequently, it is the parents who are the most distraught. Mothers tend to concentrate on the sexual aspects of the incident, and fathers are most often reacting to the attack upon their child. Parents need a great deal of supportive, caring intervention by police, medical, and counseling agencies. Again, it is strongly suggested that the focus on the child be reduced once it is determined that the child is safe and has not been physically injured. Professional psychiatric consultation is strongly recommended.

*Note*: Besides the personal experience of the author, material presented in the above sections was drawn from a variety of sources. The following references were of particular importance: 2,3,9,10,15.

## REFERENCES

1. Emergency Medicine Magazine Staff: Prescription for rape, the listening ear. Emergency Medicine, Vol. 7 No. 2, February 1975
2. Brodyaga L, Gates M, Singer S, Tucker M, White R: Rape and Its Victims: A Report For Citizens, Health Facilities, and Criminal Justice Agencies. Washington, DC; National Institute of Law Enforcement and Criminal Justice, 1975
3. Burgess AW, Holmstrom LL: Rape, Crisis and Recovery. Bowie, MD; Robert J. Brady Co., 1979
4. Groth AN, Burgess AW, Holmstrom LL: Rape: Power, Anger and Sexuality. Psychiatry Vol. 134, 1239-1243, 1977
5. Burgess AW, Holmstrom LL: Rape: Victims of Crisis. Bowie, MD; Robert J. Brady Co., 1974
6. Frederick CJ: Crisis Intervention and Emergency Mental Health. *In* Johnson WR (ed): Health In Action. New York; Holt, Rinehart and Winston, 1977
7. Gazzaniga AB, Iseri LT, Baren M: Emergency Care: Principles and Practices for the EMT-Paramedic. Reston, VA; Reston Publishing Co., Inc. 1979
8. Bard M, Ellison K: Crisis intervention and investigation of forcible rape. Police Chief. Vol. XLI No. 5, May 1974
9. Pruitt NH: Myths and misconceptions about rape. Handout material. Prince Georges County Sexual Assault Center, Prince Georges General Hospital, Cheverly, MD; 1976
10. Pruitt NH: The Grief of the Sexual Assault Victim. Paper presented to Maryland State Emergency Medical Technician Instructors— Ambulance. Field Response to Emotional Crises Workshop, Anne Arundel County, March 1979
11. Coleman JC: Psychology and Effective Behavior. Glenview, IL; Scott, Foresman and Company, 1969
12. Slaby AE, Lieb J, Tancredi LR: Handbook of Psychiatric Emergencies. Flushing, New York; Medical Examination Publishing Company, Inc., 1975
13. Parad HJ: Crisis Intervention: Selected Readings. New York, Family Service Association of America, 1965

14. Fahrney P: Sexual Assault Package: A refinement of a Previous Idea. *In* Suburban Hospital's Emergency Room procedure manual: Emergency Methods and Techniques. Suburban Hospital, Bethesda, MD
15. Wilson J: Investigation of sex crimes. *In* General Orders. Metropolitan Police, Washington, DC; General Order No. 3046, revised June 9, 1974

# CHAPTER 11

# *The Neglected, Battered, and Abused Child*

Jeffrey T. Mitchell, M.S.

## INTRODUCTION

A crying, bleeding, or burned child, or a child who appears to be emotionally rejected, has a way of getting into the very fiber of our personalities. They trigger overwhelming emotional reactions within practically any normal person.

This fact may produce serious complications in the effective and professional management of a child abuse case by emergency service personnel. It is difficult enough to handle a pediatric emergency under normal conditions. An injury that has been knowingly or willfully inflicted upon a child by an adult usually drives us into a rage, and makes us jump to the defense of the child in a manner that can occasionally cloud our clear, professional judgment.

This chapter will provide some important background information on the subject of child abuse. It will also present a variety of suggestions and guidelines that will assist the public safety personnel in making a quality assessment of the situation, and an effective intervention into the crisis. The main focus behind the intervention techniques will be a resolution of the current problem and a prevention of future incidents of child abuse within the same setting.

## BACKGROUND

### What is Child Abuse?

Child abuse is usually defined as "any physical injury or injuries" which a child (under eighteen in most states) sustains "as a result

127

of cruel or inhumane treatment" or malicious act or acts by any parent, guardian, or other person who is responsible for the custody of the child.[1] Sexual abuse is included regardless of whether or not there is physical injury. The usual criteria for determining child abuse in a court of law is that the abuse was deliberate, severe, repeated, and demonstrable (at least bruises).[2] However, more recently, some states have allowed psychological evidence in court.[3]

In some states child abuse is covered under neglect laws. Although these laws vary from state to state because of different focuses on the issue of neglect, in all fifty states a parent's physical mistreatment of a child is legally a form of neglect.[4] Neglect is generally considered to be the failure of persons responsible for the care of the child to provide the necessary food, clothing, medical care, education, sanitary environment, and emotional atmosphere conducive to growth.

## THE STATISTICS

We have no way of telling exactly how many child abuse cases there are each year. Only a portion of the actual number of cases are reported to medical, law enforcement, social service, or court agencies. Statistical researchers, however, who work with these agencies, have been able to establish some figures which point out the seriousness of the problem.

A commonly accepted figure proposed by pediatricians is that ten percent of children below the age of five who appear for treatment in hospital emergency departments were injured by their caretakers (parents, guardians, baby sitters, or others). In round numbers, then, we are talking about 150,000 cases a year in the United States.[5,6] Of the approximately 150,000 child abuse cases, it is estimated that 5,000 die of their injuries and another 30,000 a year receive permanent scars and other physical damage.[7,8]

## THE ABUSER'S PROFILE

*Any human adult has the potential to be a child abuser given the right children and the right set of circumstances.*[9]

That is a hard fact for us to accept. We do not like that potential in ourselves. We like to think of ourselves as being above this.

128

However, behavioral scientists are constantly pointing this out to us and they have some fairly convincing evidence to back up the claim. If we can keep that hard-to-swallow proposition in mind, it can help us to understand the abuser and perhaps react with some compassion instead of rage. The end results can be much more helpful for the children involved.[9]

| The Child Abuser's Profile | Remarks |
| --- | --- |
| A. Usually abusers tend to be women. | Women are abusers more frequently than men because they are home more often and for longer periods of time. |
| B. They start off as disciplining their children. | They get carried away with their anger. |
| C. Lonely or isolated. | The less the person can rely on supports in the family and the environment, the more likely they will be to abuse their children. |
| D. Victims of child abuse themselves. | They were treated badly as children themselves and they learned child abuse first hand. For many it is the only way they know to react to the frustrations and provocations of children. |
| E. Feeling worthless. | The typical child abuser does not like herself or himself and, therefore, has difficulty liking another person. As children, they were frequently told that they were bad and worthless, and they now project this onto their children. |
| F. Unsatisfied by their partners. | The child abuser generally is living within a marriage that is not fulfilling their basic needs for love and affection. |
| G. Seeking fulfillment from the child. | The child stands out as the last hope to fulfill their needs for affection. When the child is not able to live up to these heavy expectations, the child abuser strikes out in frustration. |
| H. Feeling helpless. | They do not see how someone outside the family can help them to cope with their frustrations more effectively. |
| I. Unable to cope with more crises. | The child abuser's coping skills are generally so poor as to produce problems in dealing with most routine crises. |

129

---

The following are *characteristics of mothers who are considered a high risk in abusing their children.*

---

| | | |
|---|---|---|
| A. | They demonstrate poor attention toward the baby. | They do not talk to the baby or cuddle it. Frequently they hold the baby away from them or carelessly, and they do not support the baby's head. Their general handling of the baby is somewhat rough. |
| B. | They think the baby is "ugly." | These mothers may state this feeling openly or subtly by their actions and behavior. For example, they may avoid showing their babies off or may dress the baby in such a manner as to hide the baby's features. |
| C. | They believe the baby can make adult judgments about them. | High risk mothers believe that their babies may think that they are incompetent as mothers, or make other judgments which adults might make. |
| D. | They frequently are addicted to alcohol or other drugs. | Any mother abusing drugs has a high potential to hurt her child. Her inhibitions are lowered. |
| E. | They had injured previous children. | If the pattern of child abuse with other children has been established, it is likely to continue. |
| F. | They believe the baby does not love them. | This is a crucial blow to the fragile personality of some mothers, and causes them to react irrationally toward their babies. |
| G. | They have been abandoned by the baby's father. | This eliminates an important support. The intense isolation can be overwhelming and produce a high level of frustration and consequently results in child abuse. |
| H. | They are teenage mothers. | Teenage mothers frequently lack the maturity necessary to tolerate the demands of married life or the demands of caring for a dependent infant. Frustrations build, and minor crises produce child abuse. |
| I. | They have delivered a premature or handicapped child. | This situation sometimes implies to some mothers that they are inadequate and incompetent and, therefore, cannot deliver a normal baby. If they are not mature or psychologically stable, they may strike out at their babies in anger over their perceived inadequacy.[9,10,11] |

---

## THE ABUSED CHILD'S PROFILE

A similar profile can be developed around the type of child who is more likely to be abused by his caretakers, especially his parents.

| The Abused Child's Profile | Remarks |
| --- | --- |
| A. Boys are involved more often than girls. (Sexual abuse is more common among girls.) | Boys are generally more active and more competitive, and this produces more frustration for many parents. |
| B. Demanding or dependent children. | Any child who is sick or who has special needs puts further stress on a parent and is more vulnerable to abuse. |
| C. Physically handicapped, gifted, retarded, and premature children. | They can be considered demanding and are, therefore, more vulnerable. |
| D. Illegitimate children. | Children born out of wedlock frequently point to changes in the family system. Education or work opportunities may have been given up and the parent or parents become resentful and angry. |
| E. Uncommunicative children. | Children who rarely express themselves are vulnerable because parents occasionally assume that the child is withholding information, affection, or is lying to them. |
| F. Children who are "mismatched." | Children who are not what the parents wanted are "mismatched" and can create tension. Usually the parents may have wanted a girl and had a boy, or they may have expected a quiet child and delivered a baby who was quite active. Again, frustrations build up and the child is vulnerable for abuse and neglect.[9,10,11,12] |

## WHAT CONSTITUTES A FAMILY CRISIS?

Add a serious family crisis to a situation which contains a potential abuser and an at-risk child, and you now have all the essential elements of a child abuse incident.

What constitutes a family crisis? Unemployment, overcrowding of the home, a death, a move, a birth, or property loss can trigger child abuse.[8] Even an appliance breakdown may trigger it.[9] *Child abuse* is almost always a symptom of serious family disturbance. Child abuse is just one form of a faulty family interrelationship pattern.[7,8,9]

## "THERE OUGHT TO BE A LAW"

There are laws against child abuse. In fact, every state has laws designed to provide protection for children from abuse and neglect.[12] Generally speaking, the laws provide that parents are responsible for the care of their children. In cases where this responsibility is not being fulfilled by parents, the laws provide for intervention by society.

There are four types of legal provisions for the protection of children. The first is criminal law. Then there exists juvenile court acts, protective services laws, and child abuse reporting laws.[14]

In the criminal field, there are ample laws which provide for the punishment of parents and caretakers who would murder, willfully mutilate, assault, or batter their children. New laws do not need to be developed. In extreme cases of child abuse criminal laws can be utilized to punish these horrible criminal actions. It is not easy to convict someone within the context of criminal law, and it is not always effective in child abuse cases. Proof must be available without leaving any doubt as to the criminal's guilt.[9] Prosecution ususally divides the family unit up and almost any chance of resolving the serious problems within the family system is reduced to near zero. Unfortunately, it is usually quite late when criminal law has to be evoked to protect a child. Much could have, and should have, been done before a child abuse incident became so severe as to require criminal prosecution.[4]

All states have instituted child abuse reporting laws to assure that fewer cases will go so far as to require criminal prosecution.[12] Most states provide immunity from liability for persons who report child abuse situations. Most reporting laws require all professional persons such as doctors, nurses, ambulance and police personnel, and social workers to report cases of suspected child abuse to the police or social service agencies.[1] In the majority of states, once a report is made to the police or social service agencies, they are required to investigate the complaint, offer assistance and, if assistance is refused, they may take action to secure the safety of the child by temporary removal from the home, and by bringing the family to the attention of the court system. If assistance is accepted by the family, it usually comes in the form of counseling, group therapy, protective supervision of the child within the family, and the teaching of new coping skills.[5,7,13]

Child-abusing parents can be helped by such programs.[10] They are not beyond help. Most programs around the nation report a good problem resolution rate with parents who receive help especially if they accept it willingly.[7]

If the courts must enter the picture because of a family's refusal of outside intervention, the courts have a variety of options depending on the states in which they are working. They may temporarily or permanently remove a child from the home, order counseling, protective supervision, or further medical and psychiatric intervention.[4]

It should be noted that the removal of a child from a family on a permanent basis is an extreme action by the courts, and is usually done only after careful consideration of all aspects of the case. This action carries with it some inherent dangers. The family unit is split and children often have severe difficulties adjusting to the demands of a new environment. Children generally do not wish to be removed from the family; they simply want the painful treatment they are undergoing to stop.[9]

The real emphasis in treatment should be focused on the parents and not the children. Treating parents allows children to stay within the family, but in a safer, healthier environment.


## SEXUAL ABUSE

Additional details on sexual abuse are presented in the chapter on sexual assault (see Chapter Ten). At this point, however, it should suffice to say that parents who sexually abuse their children are demonstrating clear symptoms of severe emotional distress within the family system. The focus should be on the parents and not the child because it is a problem that belongs to the parents. Between 200,000 and 500,000 cases of sexual abuse of children occur each year in the United States.[12]

There are two types of sexual abuse. The first is the seduction type in which the youngster is enticed or entrapped into sexual activity with the parent (or guardian or relative). There is little danger of physical punishment, but a great danger of long term psychological damage. The second type of sexual abuse is that in which the child is forced into sexual activity and maintained in it by threats and fear. The child in this situation is more vulnerable to physical injury. The physical abuse frequently makes the youngster known to police or social service agencies or to the medical professional. Faster intervention by outside agencies reduces the likelihood of long term psychological damage.

Parents who receive help for their emotional problems improve and they stop sexually abusing their children.[7,10] Crisis workers must commit themselves to helping these unfortunate people, and not to their punishment which neither cures them nor serves any useful purpose.

## ASSESSMENT

Proper evaluation of a child abuse incident is the key to the delivery of the appropriate intervention, and the development of the most helpful referral source. The following guidelines will be most helpful to the emergency service personnel who are dispatched to the scene of a potential child abuse situation, and who are faced with the assessment of the problem.

- Physical abuse should almost always be considered whenever a child has been injured and the cause of the injury is not obvious.[12]
- The younger a child is, the less likely it is that injuries occurred accidentally.
- Make a slow approach to the child.
- A visual assessment is always first in priority.
- Do not touch the child (except to provide basic life saving first aid) until you have established rapport.
- Watch the child. Focus on what he or she does. Observations can frequently tell you much more than the child's words. (Besides, children under three years of age have such poorly developed vocabulary that they usually do not communicate well.)
- Talk directly to the child in a very gentle tone.
- Get on the same physical level. Bend, crouch down, kneel, or sit if you are not at his eye level.
- Gather as much information from the parents as possible.
- Parents should be interviewed separately. "Mrs. _____ can you tell me what happened here?"[14,15]

## WHAT TO LOOK FOR

The following will provide some clues to child abuse:

- Obvious bruises, welts, or burns on the child's skin.
- The child may be dressed inappropriately for the weather.

134

- The child appears withdrawn or in a daydreaming state.
- The child exhibits excessive fear, but does not pull away from treatment. (Many children are beaten more severely for pulling away from a parent, so they learn to stand still when someone is about to hurt or, as in the case of a crisis worker, help.)
- A key symptom is the absence of selectivity. Children generalize about their world. Mom and Dad have brought them pain so they make an assumption that everyone will treat them the same. They expect all adults to hurt them. Many times children will be very affectionate to a stranger (for example, a rescuer or a police officer). They believe all adults will eventually turn against them so they attempt to get whatever they can that is good in the relationship before it turns sour. When you see a child who is just *too* affectionate to you as a stranger you should think, "serious possibility of child abuse."
- The child is too dirty and unkept.
- A child is removed from a burning house and his parents, guardians, or baby sitter are nowhere to be found.
- The child has signs of many other injuries in various stages of healing.
- There may have been frequent prior runs to the same household for the same injured child.
- An infant with an obvious break in a long bone is a suspected child abuse victim. Infant bones are too pliable and rarely break without excessive external force.[9]
- The child may cry constantly and not be consoled by any adults present.
- An infant with a closed head injury has a characteristic shrill, high pitched cry.[12]
- In an infant, the "soft spot" on top of the head may be swollen from increased pressure inside the skull from a closed head injury, or it may be sunk in if the child has not been nourished properly.
- The child may have clumps of hair missing from his head where his hair has been pulled out. There may be bruises by the lips where he was gagged. Cigarette burns, tie marks, and iron burns may be present. Other characteristic marks may be present.
- There may be evidence of malnutrition such as swollen

135

abdomen, wasted buttocks, and a vacant stare in the child's eyes.

## THE INTERVIEW OF THE CHILD [9]

- Interview the child alone if possible.
- Be aware that the child may lie to protect his parents. He only has one Mom and Dad and he will do whatever he feels is necessary to make sure that nothing happens to them.[9] A case in point was an incident that occurred in which an ambulance attendant walked into a house and found a man in the process of severely beating his four-year-old son. The rescue worker was so infuriated that he attacked the man and was beating him up when the child squeezed in between the two men and pleaded with the ambulance attendant not to hurt his daddy.
- No accusations should be made.
- The child should simply be asked once to tell you what happened.
- No interrogation should take place.
- The child should not be accused of lying or withholding information. He may be too fearful to speak, or may think that he will get his parents into trouble and they may be taken away.
- Ask only questions that are pertinent to his immediate care and safety.[12,14,15]
- If you are a police officer and find it necessary to question the child further to establish a clear case of child abuse, the following items have been added to assist you:
    - A. Do not accuse the child's parents.
    - B. Be nonjudgmental.
    - C. Interview the child alone, not with the parents present.
    - D. Follow the questioning outline described below.

*Note:* This line of questioning begins with a non-threatening question and proceeds to more serious questions designed to bring out hints as to the treatment of children. No one question gives conclusive evidence, but helps to establish a trend. Adjust your vocabulary to the age of the child.

136

1. "What does your Mommy look like?"
2. "What kind of Mommy is she?"
3. "Is she a happy Mommy or a sad Mommy?"
4. "Is Mommy angry a lot?"
5. "What does Mommy like about you?"
6. "What kinds of things does Mommy dislike about you?"
7. "What does your Mommy do when she likes something about you?"
8. "How about when she doesn't like something about you, what does she do then?"
9. "Can you describe yourself to me? What kind of a little girl or boy are you?"
10. "What do you think are the best things about you?"
11. "What are the not so good things about yourself?"
12. "What does Mommy do if you do one of those things?"
13. "Can you tell me the difference between a spanking and a beating?"
14. Officers should ask specific questions regarding sexual suspicions. For example, the officer might ask if the child knows what daddy's penis looks like when he is going to the bathroom and at other times. Also, ask about any specific sexual acts. Be careful to make sure the language chosen is understandable to the child. The best way to do this is to ask the child to name his or her own body parts and use the same wording to ask the questions in this section.
15. "If there was one thing that could be different about Mommy or Daddy, what would you wish that could be?"[9]

This line of questioning could be used to ask the child about Daddy also. Repeating the questions and substituting the word "Dad" or "Daddy" for "Mom" or "Mommy" is often helpful.

*Note:* This depth of questioning is not necessary by ambulance and fire personnel. It is only used by police and hospital personnel to establish a clear case for court prosecution or social service action. Likewise, the parents should be interviewed carefully by police officers who are attempting to establish a criminal case or a social service referral.

## THE PARENTS' INTERVIEW[9]

A. Interview parents separately and not in the presence of the child.
B. Be nonjudgmental.
C. Avoid making accusations.
D. Follow this interview outline:

1. "Mrs. _____, how would you describe this particular child?"
2. "How about each of your other children?"
   (Officers should note significant differences; they are good clues to how this parent views the child and the expectations they may have of that child.)
3. "Do you think this child has any special function in your family?"
4. "Is there any need that he fulfills better than the others?"
5. "What were your own parents like?", "How did they treat you?"
6. "Describe yourself as a parent."
7. "What is your relationship with your husband like?"
8. "Has their been any significant changes in your family lately?"
9. "What are the biggest problems in your family?"
10. "How much alcohol is used in this family?"
11. "Do you have any relatives or friends nearby?"
12. "Some of the information we've gathered so far leaves some questions in our minds which we would like to clear up. Many, many parents get frustrated when they are lonely and having problems like the ones you are facing now. Occasionally, they lose control a little and strike their children. Most of the time they need some help with their problems, but don't know where or how to get it. Has anything like that ever happened to you?"
13. Any additional questions can now be added and questioning can become more specific.
14. The father in the family can be interviewed in a similar fashion.[9]

Your suspicions should be aroused if the stories about the child do not match up, if there appears to be a delay in calling for assistance, or if the parents seem uncooperative and evasive.[18]

(Material in the interview of the child and the parent's interview has been adapted for use with the permission of the author, Nancy Hall Pruitt, President, A and T of Virginia, Inc., Springfield, VA.)

## CRISIS INTERVENTION TECHNIQUES

- The first responsibility of crisis workers is to assure the safety of the youngster.
- This is most easily achieved by transporting the injured child to the hospital in an ambulance.
- If the parents refuse to cooperate, the police should be called to the scene to secure the child and begin an investigation.
- The expression of anger (the loss of one's "cool" on the part of the crisis worker) is counterproductive and may do much more harm than good.
- No pictures should be taken of the child except by police officers who are responsible for the establishment of evidence for court prosecution.
- Undressing of a child abuse victim should be done only as much as facilitates a good physical assessment and proper medical care.
- If at all possible, a caring and sensitive female should be assigned to the ambulance crew. If a female police officer is available she may be most helpful in dealing with the frightened youngster.
- Be as compassionate and sympathetic to parents as possible. It helps to assure continued cooperation from them.
- Document on the records all factual information and be sure that the proper hospital personnel are aware of all facts and suspicions.
- Whenever possible, refer the parents to agencies such as social services who have programs to help the child abusing parents.

The above material was drawn primarily from the following references: 5,7,9,10,12,13,15,19,20.

## CAUTIONS

There are three major cautions that should be noted regarding child abuse situations:

A. Vomiting alone is *not* a good indicator of child abuse. Many children vomit after a variety of injuries and a good number would vomit when excited or frightened.[12]

B. Although child abuse is usually considered when a child has multiple injuries in various body systems, victims of auto accidents frequently have multiple injuries and should not necessarily be treated as a child abuse case unless there appears to be extenuating evidence. For the most part, an auto accident victim should be treated as an auto accident victim and any suspicions beyond that should be stated to the hospital personnel so that further investigation can be pursued.

C. Sudden infant death cases should not be confused with child abuse. Accusations of neglect made to the parents of a sudden infant death child may do irreparable psychological damage. A sudden infant death case usually shows no signs of neglect. The parents are appropriately distressed. The infant's body usually appears clean and well cared for and there are no bruises, swellings, or marks that would indicate abuse. However, in some cases, pooling of deoxygenated blood in the tissues can easily be mistaken for bruises. If you are in doubt, treat the death of a baby as a sudden infant death and relay any suspicions to hospital personnel or to the police. (See Chapter 13, the section on Sudden Infant Death Syndrome.)

### REFERENCES

1. Annotated Code of Maryland, Article 27, Section 35A, 1974
2. Parker B: Family violence: Its victims, its recognition. Presented at a seminar on Family Violence, Maryland Nurses Association, 1978.
3. Rosenberg, LA: "Psychological Assessment of the Battered Child. A workshop presented by Johns Hopkins Hospital, Department of Pediatrics. Baltimore, March 2, 1979
4. Paulsen MG: Legal protections against child abuse. Children, Vol. 13, 1966

5. Helfer RE: Helping the Battered Child and His Family. Philadelphia, Lippincott Publishing Co., 1972
6. Helfer, RE: The world of abnormal rearing. Pediatric Basics, Issue No. 11, 1974
7. Irwin T: To combat child abuse and neglect. *In* Bard M: The Function of the Police in Crisis Intervention and Conflict Management. Washington, DC; Criminal Justice Associates, 1975
8. Coleman JC: Battered children. Psychology and Effective Behavior, Glenview, IL; Scott, Foresman and Company, 1969
9. Pruitt, NH: The child abuse problem. Address delivered to Maryland Nurses Association at a seminar on Family Violence, 1978
10. Batterton R: Child abuse, fact and fiction. Pamphlet distributed by the Maryland Department of Human Resources, 1978
11. Osborn C: Profile of the 'typical' abusing parent. Pamphlet distributed by the College of General Studies, University of South Carolina, 1977
12. Gazzaniga AB: Iseri, LT, Baren M: Emergency Care Principles and Practices for the EMT-Paramedic. Reston, VA; Reston Publishing Company, Inc., 1979
13. Professional Standards Division of the International Association of Chiefs of Police: Child abuse. Training Key No. 207, Gaithersburg, MD; International Association of Chiefs of Police, 1974
14. Pitcher RA: The police. *In* Kempe CH, Helfer RE: Helping the Battered Child and His Family. Philadelphia, Lippincott Publishing Co., 1972
15. Professional Standards Division of the International Association of Chiefs of Police: Interviewing the Child Sex Victim. Training Key No. 224, Gaithersburg, MD; International Association of Chiefs of Police, 1974
16. Baltimore County Police: Child abuse check list, physical findings. A flyer prepared by and distributed by the Baltimore County Police Department, Youth Division, Baltimore County, Maryland, 1976
17. Baltimore County Police: Child abuse and neglect, what to look for. A flyer prepared and distributed by the Baltimore County Police Department, Youth Division, Baltimore County, Maryland, 1976
18. Baltimore County Police: Child abuse, look for these signs. A flyer prepared and distributed by the Baltimore County Police Department, Youth Division, Baltimore County, Maryland, 1976
19. Burgess AW, Holmstrom LL: The police. *In* Rape: Crisis and Recovery. Bowie, MD; Robert J. Brady Co., 1979
20. Burgess AW, Holstrom LL, McCausland MP: Child sexual assault by family member. Rape: Crisis and Recovery. Bowie, MD; Robert J. Brady Co., 1979

# CHAPTER **12**

# Suicide

## Lawrence D. Messier, M. A.

### INTRODUCTION

Suicide may be the least investigated and most misunderstood form of human behavior. Societal attitudes toward suicide vary from culture to culture, and from situation to situation. While some societies have praised suicidal acts (such as those of Kamikaze pilots), most societies condemn suicide and view it as a deplorable act which is seldom talked about openly. The mere mention of suicide is likely to evoke emotional responses and personal reactions from most people. For these reasons, suicide has become a mysterious and threatening act. It is perhaps the single crisis situation most people, including crisis intervention personnel, are least prepared to manage.[1]

The lack of understanding the nature of suicide can easily be seen in the following list of common misconceptions about suicidal behavior.[2]

| | FALSE | TRUE |
|---|---|---|
| 1. | People who talk about suicide do not commit suicide. | Of any ten people who kill themselves, eight have given definite warnings. |
| 2. | Suicide happens without warning. | The suicidal person gives many clues and warnings about his or her intention. |
| 3. | Suicidal people are very intent on dying. | Most are undecided about living or dying. They usually gamble with death, leaving it to others to save them. |
| 4. | Once a person attempts suicide he or she is suicidal forever. | Usually people who wish to kill themselves are suicidal only for a limited period of time. |
| 5. | Suicide occurs among the rich more than the poor. | Suicide is represented proportionately among all levels of society. |

| FALSE | TRUE |
|---|---|
| 6. All suicidal individuals are mentally ill or psychotic. | Although suicidal individuals may be very sad they are not necessarily mentally ill. |

## BACKGROUND

Suicide is indeed a serious problem. There are at least 2,000,000 people living in this country who have attempted suicide at least once.[3] A suicide attempt occurs once every minute in the United States.[4] Twice as many people die from suicide than from homicides, and at least 70 percent of the population have thought about suicide to some degree. The annual cost to state and local agencies for emergency medical treatment, hospitalization, and loss of income for suicide related incidents is estimated at four billion dollars per year.[5] Many of these attempted and completed suicides can be prevented. Competent and sensitive professional intervention may very well mean the difference between life and death.[4] The remainder of this chapter will provide a basic understanding of suicidal behavior and guidelines for intervention.

## DEFINITIONS

To enable better understanding of background material on suicide a few important terms will be defined.

1. *Suicide*—the intended act of self inflicted death.[6]
2. *Ambivalence*—the simultaneous existence in an individual of two opposite feelings or attitudes.[7] In respect to suicide, it refers to the state of mixed emotions about taking one's life. Even in the most serious suicidal individual there is some feeling of the desire to live.[1]
3. *Lethality*—the potential of a given method of suicide for ending the individual's life. Lethality is rated by the length of time between the initiation of the act and the occurrence of death.[2]

144

4. *Social Isolation*—the pattern of avoiding social contacts.[7]
5. *Social Integration*—can be considered the opposite of social isolation. It is a situation in which people have shared feelings, interest in each other, and common goals.[8]

## INCIDENCE

As previously mentioned, suicide occurs more often than most people realize. Normally each year, for every 100,000 people, there are 110 suicide attempts. Recent statistics suggest that there may have been an increase in suicide over the last ten years. Figures indicate an increased rate of suicide in the 15 to 24 year age group, a 49 percent increase in white females and an 80 percent increase in non-white females. Some mental health workers believe that suicide is underreported by physicians and others in an attempt to spare families the agony of public exposure. If this is true, the problem of suicide may be even greater.[8,9]

## WHO

It is difficult to answer the question of "who" commits or attempts suicide because there is no one particular kind of person who resorts to suicide. Suicide occurs in all races, creeds, ages, sexes, and cultures. Males *commit* suicide three times as often as females, while females *attempt* suicide three times as often as males.[3,8] The suicide rate is lowest among married individuals, higher among the widowed, and highest among those who are divorced or separated. Suicide below age fifteen is seldom reported, but has been known to occur. Blacks have a lower rate of suicide than do whites.[3,8,9,10]

## HOW

The particular method chosen by an individual to carry out the suicide is important, especially in regard to emergency intervention. The relative lethality of the method chosen will determine how quickly the crisis intervention worker must react and aid in the emergency assessment of the suicidal individual. The greater the lethality, the more determined the individual is likely to be to end his or her life, and the more crucial proper intervention becomes. One survey of mental health workers ranked the following common methods of self injury in order of their lethality: [2]

1. Firearms and explosives.
2. Jumping.
3. Cutting vital organs.
4. Hanging.
5. Drowning (cannot swim).
6. Poison (solid and liquid).
7. Cutting non-vital organs.
8. Drowning (can swim).
9. Poisoning (gases).
10. Analgesic substances (pain medications).

## WHY

The thought of suicide crosses almost everyone's mind at some point in life. However, most people do not act on the thought and find other ways to deal with frustrating and painful situations. What is it then that drives some people to choose suicide as a way of coping with their problems? There is no single causative factor or situation which can explain all suicides. Suicide is an extremely personal and individual act. The situations, feelings, and thoughts which lead to suicide are complex and unique to each individual. However, there are theories which aid in understanding why people commit suicide. Listed below are five patterns of suicide. They are derived from various theories and are not meant to explain every suicidal pattern, but they do explain some common factors seen in many suicides. [3,4,8,11]

1. *The Impulsive Suicide.* This pattern of suicide often occurs after some major disappointment or frustration such as a failure to achieve a promotion, a business failure, failure to gain admission to professional school, or failure to achieve some important personal goal. The failure results in a major blow to the individual's pride, self-esteem, and confidence. The humiliation and embarrassment are too great for the individual to bear and suicide becomes a way to end the situation without prolonged suffering.

146

2. *The Depressed Suicide.* This pattern is seen when the individual is seriously depressed. The depression may be long standing or recent in onset. In such a state the individual finds no meaning, purpose, or happiness in life and feels that the present situation will not change. The person is so depressed as to be unable to realize that his feelings about the worthlessness of life are temporary and due to the depressed condition. The future is seen as hopeless and, since life is not worth living, suicide becomes the only alternative.

3. *Suicide as an Escape From Suffering.* In this pattern, suicide becomes a way of escaping from intolerable pain and anguish. The pain may be caused by a serious physical illness such as cancer or some other debilitating disease, especially if the disease is likely to be terminal. The suffering may also be part of an emotional disorder in which the individual feels there will be no improvement, and the despair of such a situation is overwhelming. The prospect of continuing life under these circumstances is unbearable and the individual decides to end the suffering by suicide.

4. *The Communication Suicide.* This pattern of suicide behavior is one in which the individual does not desire to end his life as much as to change the way other people act toward him. The attempted suicide is a way of communicating some message to an important and valued person in the individual's life. The individual may seek to gain the sympathy, affection, and understanding of a loved one, which could not be obtained in other ways, by a dramatic attempt on his own life. The message may also be one of guilt, where the individual attempts suicide to evoke great guilt on the part of someone who has rejected or deprived him.

The message may be hostile and angry. The suicide attempt may have been meant to embarrass and hurt someone whom the individual feels has caused his present frustrations. Suicide becomes a way of saying, "You'll be sorry" in a dramatic way.

5. *Loss of a Loved One.* This pattern involves the loss of someone very close and important. The loss is most commonly caused by death, but may also be seen in divorce or physical separation. While the loss is usually recent it may have occurred at some previous time in the individual's life. The person lost is usually a spouse, parent, sibling, or a very close friend. Life with-

out the lost person is full of loneliness and meaninglessness. The continued absence of the important person evokes greater sadness and a desire for reunion with this person. Suicide is seen almost magically as a way to achieve reunion with the lost loved one in death. This may be seen in older individuals who attempt suicide on the birthday or date of the death of a deceased spouse.

## EMOTIONAL STATE

A good understanding and acceptance of the feelings experienced by suicidal persons is the most valuable tool for effective intervention in a crisis situation involving suicide. It should be remembered that although the feelings of the suicidal individual may seem extreme or exaggerated, these feelings are real and are felt intensely by such individuals. In short, suicidal individuals are in great emotional pain. The emotions discussed here may occur in combination and may vary in intensity from one individual to the next.

Most suicidal people experience profound feelings of hopelessness, helplessness, and worthlessness. They feel that there is no way out of the present, unbearable situation (helplessness) and that the future holds no hope for change in the situation (hopelessness). They also feel that they have no value as persons (worthless). Although the true nature of the situation may be that, with help from others, the crisis situation can be resolved; the suicidal individual often has difficulty directly asking for help. He also has difficulty realizing that help is needed to solve his problems. The suicidal individual may not feel the strength to seek help because he is so depressed.

The social isolation common among suicidal individuals often results in a lack of friends, family, and other sources of help and support. They feel separated from other people and often have few friends and poor relationships with their families. They expect rejection and unrewarding experiences with other people. Loneliness and despair from this social isolation is common.[8]

Adolescents who attempt suicide often feel, and openly display, feelings of internal anger. These feelings include hate and bitterness toward another person who may have rejected or hurt them in some way. These hostile feelings may be quite intense and may drive the young person to a suicidal act.[4,8]

Depression is present in most suicidal individuals. In addition, to the hopelessness and helplessness previously mentioned, there may be feelings of loss of energy, lack of meaning in life, and great emotional pain.[6,8]

A feeling present in almost all suicidal individuals is a state of ambivalence. Even the most determined suicidal individual has mixed feelings about death. Regardless of the seriousness of a person's suicide threats, there is always some desire to survive. This can often be seen in the individual's hopes and fantasies about being rescued prior to death. The hidden and suppressed desire to live, on the part of suicidal individuals, will be a major focus of crisis intervention.[1,11]

## THOUGHT PROCESSES

The thinking of suicidal individuals is marked by two qualities: *rigidity* and *extremeness*. The rigidity of suicidal thinking can be called "either-or" thinking. Situations and people tend to be seen as good or bad, or black and white, with no middle ground. The lack of flexibility in such thinking results in a "tunnel vision" which prevents the individual from seeing many alternatives to the present situation other than suicide. The extremeness of suicidal thought may be seen in exaggerations of fears, common to all people. A relatively minor illness or required surgery may be interpreted as terminal. A failure to achieve some personal goal may be interpreted as a failure of life in general. This extreme thinking at times may extend to the need to live a perfect life or commit suicide.[1,18]

## PRECIPITATING EVENTS

While some suicides may occur without apparent reason, many can be precipitated or triggered by a specific event or events in the individual's recent past. Awareness of these common precipitating events will greatly aid in emergency assessment in a suicidal crisis. Some frequently observed precipitating events are listed below.[1,3,4,8]

GENERAL:
1. Diagnosis of major illness.
2. Loss of a loved one (family, spouse, or child).
3. Termination of a close relationship.
4. Economic loss (foreclosure, bankruptcy).
5. Threat of arrest or incarceration.

MEN:

WOMEN:

ADOLESCENT:

      6. Divorce or separation.
      7. Social isolation.
      8. Downward change in social status.
      9. Failure to achieve personal goals.

MEN:      1. Vocational failure (promotion).
      2. Loss of job.

WOMEN:  1. Loss of personal relationship (spouse, lover, or child).

ADOLESCENT: 1. Family problems.
      2. Failure to achieve grades or school success.
      3. Acceptance into social groups.
      4. Humiliation in presence of peers.
      5. Loss of loved friend or relative.

ELDERLY (More likely a long-standing situation than recent event):

      1. Loneliness and social isolation.
      2. Being a burden on others.
      3. Feeling unwanted.
      4. Loss of spouse.
      5. Forced retirement.
      6. Financial problems.

## CLUES TO SUICIDAL THOUGHT

In some crisis situations the potential for suicide may not be immediately apparent. Suicide may be a part or a result of other crisis situations. If potentially suicidal individuals can be identified before any attempt at self injury, assistance may be provided before the situation becomes dangerous. Remember, 80 percent of suicides communicate their suicidal intentions prior to any attempt. To aid in the detection of potential suicidal behavior, a list of common clues to suicide are presented.[1,3,4,8,11]

1. Sudden changes in an individual's personality, habits, and attitudes.
2. Marked depression, sleeplessness, agitation, tension, nervousness, loss of energy.
3. Difficulty in concentrating or thinking clearly.
4. Increasing social isolation, loss of interest in former friends and activities.

5. Noticeable decline in job or school performance.
6. Neglect of personal appearance and hygiene.
7. Preparing affairs for death (making of wills, buying large insurance policies, giving away prized possessions).
8. Suicide threats, even in subtle form:
   "I just cannot take any more."
   "They would be better off without me."
   "I won't be around much longer for you to put up with me."
   "You'll be sorry . . . "
9. Lack of concern for personal welfare: "Who cares about me anyhow?"

## SPECIAL CAUTIONS

1. Take every suicide threat seriously. The majority of individuals who commit suicide have previously threatened or attempted suicide. Any threat must be taken seriously because the next attempt may be the final one.[3,4]
2. The impact of a suicidal situation on emergency service personnel may be powerful. It may arouse great anxiety and fears of being unable to cope with the crisis. It may also arouse memories in the intervener of times when he or she felt in a similiar manner. If the situation becomes too disturbing, call in assistance and allow someone else to take over. Your confidence and sensitivity are your most important tools in preventing suicide.[1,3]
3. There is frequently a homicidal component to a suicidal threat. A suicidal person may attempt to take someone with him. Great caution is necessary when trying to help a person threatening suicide.

## EMERGENCY ASSESSMENT OF SELF DESTRUCTIVE POTENTIAL

The main task of assessment in respect to suicide is to determine, as best as possible, the potential for immediate and lethal suicidal behavior on the part of the individual. While every potential suicidal situation contains great risk, some factors increase the risk of suicide substantially. Listed below are the crucial factors which suggest immediate and serious danger of suicide.[1,2]

### Emergency Assessment Scheme

| Factor | Very High Risk |
| --- | --- |
| 1. Age. | Males over 35.<br>Elderly. |
| 2. Method. | Immediately available.<br>High lethality. |
| 3. Onset of self destructive behavior. | Previous attempt. |
| 4. Alcohol. | Chronic abuse or present intoxication. |
| 5. Precipitating events. | Loss of loved one.<br>Loss of job.<br>Threat of arrest, prosecution.<br>Chronic or serious illness.<br>Anticipated surgery. |
| 6. Resources: Personal (family, friends), other (social, community, financial). | Limited or absent. |
| 7. Social Integration—Isolation. | Isolation. |
| 8. Emotional background. | Chronic emotional disturbance, instability. |
| 9. Individual's present state. | Uncommunicative.<br>Distorted and disorganized thinking.<br>Depressed, hostile. |

## INTERVENTION

Most suicidal crises are temporary. Intervention to prevent suicide must be started without hesitation, and proceed with great patience and flexibility. Due to the individual nature of each crisis situation, no set of techniques can be effective in all cases. The crisis worker must be flexible enough in his or her approach to adapt to the individual and the situation. A general step by step intervention guide is provided below. It contains techniques found most successful by experts in the field of suicide.[1,4,5,11]

> STEP 1: Make the environment safe, isolate the individual from further tension and provocation. Move to a private area if possible.

STEP 2: Build a trusting relationship.

    A. Tell the individual who you are and that you are trying to help. (Only one rescuer should work directly with the suicidal person. Second and third rescuers remain silent, but present.)

    B. Let the individual know that you take his or her threat seriously.

    C. Listen with interest and sensitivity and let the individual know by responding with comments like these: "I can see that this is really a difficult situation" or, "You seem to be overwhelmed by these things. I would like to help you."

    D. Be careful not to argue with the way a person feels. Attend to and respond to the emotions behind the words: "That must have made you very sad" or, "I understand why you feel so lonely." This is called validating feelings. Validating means that the person is given the message that it is okay to have and express whatever feelings he has.

    E. Do not hesitate to talk about the individual's plan for suicide. Rapport and trust occurs when the intervener is comfortable talking with the individual and vice versa.

    F. Expect the individual to question your sincerity and desire to help. Reaffirm your desire to help as one person to another.

    G. Offer food, candy, cigarettes to the person.

STEP 3: Evaluate the suicide potential using the emergency assessment scheme described previously.

STEP 4: Try to gain more information about the individual and the problems which have caused his present feelings. Address yourself to the life side of the individual's ambivalent feelings and offer support and encouragement.

STEP 5: Focus on the main problem or, if more than one exists, address each problem one at a time.

STEP 6: Consider with the individual alternative solutions to his problem. Suicidal individuals are usually rigid in their thinking and may not have considered other alternatives. Be flexible and optimistic but do not lie or promise anything you cannot deliver.

STEP 7: Try to arrive at specific actions which the individual agrees with. Obtain the support of family and close friends, if possible, and consider other resources.

STEP 8: Immediate referral to hospital or other protective environment.

STEP 9. In the unfortunate situation in which the person has succeeded in committing suicide, crisis intervention efforts should be directed at the survivors.[2]

## DO NOT:

1. Dismiss a suicidal threat or challenge the individual to, "Go ahead and do it."
2. Moralize or tell the individual he is wrong and should be ashamed. This will prevent the establishment of a trusting relationship and may provoke the individual to suicide.
3. Try to analyze or interpret the "hidden" reasons for individual's behavior.
4. Move too quickly. Helping a suicidal person takes time.
5. Take unnecessary risks.

*NOTE:* Sometimes, depite all efforts, someone may succeed in taking their own life. Crisis workers need to be assured that this is always a possibility in spite of their efforts to handle the case as carefully as possible according to the guidelines in this and other books. Every human being is unique and no human behavior is exactly predictable. No intervention techniques can assure 100 percent success. Good techniques may only increase the probability of success.

The loss of a person to suicide is a crushing blow to many crisis workers. They need to express their feelings of depression, loss, and disappointment in themselves and their efforts to help. But they should not take these unfortunate losses personally. Nothing they, or anyone else, might have done could have changed the outcome of the incident if the suicidal person was intent on accomplishing self destruction.

## REFERENCES

1. Hatton CL, Valenti SM, Rink A: Suicide: Assessment and Intervention. New York, Appleton-Century-Crofts, 1977
2. Faberow N, Shneidman E (eds): The Cry for Help. New York, McGraw-Hill, 1965
3. Grollman EA: Suicide. Boston, Beacon Press, 1971
4. Shneidman E, Farberow N: Clues to Suicide. New York, McGraw-Hill, 1957
5. Frederick CJ, Lague L: Dealing with the crisis of suicide. Public Affairs Pamplet No. 406A, Public Affairs Committee Inc., New York, 1972
6. Flach FF, Draghi SC: The Nature and Treatment of Depression. New York, Wiley and Sons, 1975
7. Chaplin JP: Dictionary of Psychology. New York, Dell Publishing Company, 1975
8. Lester G, Lester D: Suicide: The Gamble with Death. Englewood Cliffs, NJ; Prentice-Hall, Inc., 1971
9. Maris RW: Social Forces in Urban Suicide. Homewood, IL; Dorsey Press, 1969
10. Merton RK, Nisbet RA: Contemporary Social Problems. New York; Harcourt, Brace and World, 1966
11. Freedman AM, Kaplan HI, Saddock BJ: Modern Synopsis of Comprehensive Textbook of Psychiatry, II. Baltimore, Williams and Wilkins, 1976

# CHAPTER 13

# Special Problems

Jeffrey T. Mitchell, M.S., Clark J. Hudak, M.S.W.

## INTRODUCTION

A book of this size cannot adequately address every conceivable type of crisis. Many of the crisis intervention guidelines presented in the preceding chapters can easily be applied by the reader to other situations which have not been specifically described here.

There are, however, some crises which require particular knowledge and sensitivity by the crisis worker. This chapter will provide emergency service personnel with background information and intervention skills for managing crises involving the aged, sudden infant death, and terminal illness.

## THE AGED

For the purposes of this chapter, an aged person may be defined as one who is sixty-five years old or older. It should be carefully noted, however, that chronological age is a very inaccurate indicator of a person's physical or mental status. Many old people are very active both physically and mentally. Chronological age alone does not imply inactivity, senility, or poor health. Only five percent of all elderly people are in poor enough health to be in hospitals and nursing homes. The rest are leading active and productive lives in the community.

Since 1900, when the average life expectancy was forty-seven, there has been a twenty-five year expansion of average life expectancy for Americans to age seventy-two. In 1900, only four percent of the population was above sixty-five. Today, twenty-two million people, or ten percent of US citizens are over sixty-five and the percentage is expected to rise in the next decade.[1]

The elderly often have a sense of satisfaction with their lives and remain productive through most of their years beyond age sixty-five. They have to face a set of problems, however, that are quite unlike any of the problems they worked through in earlier stages of development. Emergency service personnel who become familiar with the problems and special needs of the elderly are more likely to be successful in assisting old people in times of crises.

## The Problems Of The Aged

Elderly people face a host of problems which are summarized in the following paragraphs.

### Physical Appearance

As people grow older their physical appearance gradually changes. Among other things, their hair grays, their skin wrinkles, and they experience changes in posture. The ears and nose become elongated as cartilage continues to grow while bones and skin have decreased in growth. Eyesight and hearing often fade in old age. Frequently old people are very sensitive to the changes that have taken place in their bodies. Crisis workers need to be careful not to joke about or unnecessarily discuss these changes.

### Emotional Changes

Some elderly people experience slowed thinking, forgetfulness, rigid thought patterns, and irritability. They may be anxious about their security. They also become depressed and feel a loss of social status connected to the retirement from their jobs and a lowered financial status. Grief is common in the elderly who have lost loved ones, jobs, good health, and the ability to be active and independent.

### Death Of a Spouse

The death of a spouse often is linked to a decline in health and functioning in the surviving partner. In most cases, the loss of a spouse is the single most serious loss that elderly people face. The effects of bereavement can remain for many years.

## Problems In Marriage

Many elderly people have more conflict with their spouses after the children leave the home and/or after they are retired. The increased contact may be responsible in part for this conflict. If the elderly do not have adequate interests to keep them involved they may more easily "get on each other's nerves."

Sexual difficulties often increase, especially if there has been surgery or if the couple is overly anxious regarding declining sexual urges. Frequently couples avoid sexual contact out of a fear of heart attack or stroke. Lowered affection and sexual contact may, in some cases, produce more marital conflict.

## Retirement

The forced retirement of many elderly people often gives them a sense of worthlessness and obsolescence, especially if their jobs have been replaced by machines. Some old people feel so depressed over the loss of their jobs that they may lose their desire to live. Suicide risks increase in the elderly. Twenty-five percent of *all* suicides are among people sixty-five or older.[1]

## Sensory Loss

For many elderly, a decline in the sense of sight, hearing, and smell intensifies their feelings of helplessness and hopelessness. They may also feel a bit more suspicious of people around them who they cannot see or hear too well. Unfortunately, many people assume that a person who hears or sees poorly is intellectually inferior. Crisis workers would be making a serious mistake to assume that an elderly person is "stupid" because he does not hear or see as well as other people.

## COMMON EMOTIONAL REACTIONS TO THE PROBLEMS OF GROWING OLD

The aged generally experience a number of emotional reactions:

- Grief over the loss of loved ones, job, status, or other events.
- Guilt over things they wanted to accomplish but failed to, and also over things they wish they had not done.
- Loneliness.
- Depression.
- Anxiety.
- A sense of helplessness and vulnerability.
- Anger and frustration over problems that they cannot solve.
- Fear—over crimes directed against them, loss of control of one's own functions (physical and social), impending death, financial problems, and other problems.

## CRISIS INTERVENTION SKILLS

The guidelines listed here should be helpful to crisis workers who come into contact with elderly people.

- Be aware that old people often find it difficult to ask for help because of their sense of pride and personal privacy. Do not belittle them if they do ask for help.
- Many of the elderly in the nation were immigrants who never learned English. Utilize family members, friends, or neighbors to help with communication problems.
- To properly evaluate the current problem, the crisis worker needs a good working knowledge of the person's history and life situations.
- Old people frequently have a sense of "immediacy" about them. That is, they feel that they will die or that something horrible will happen to them if the crisis worker does not take quick action. They may become demanding if they feel very threatened by the problems. Quick response to the pleas for help from the elderly should be made when possible and appropriate.

160

- Touching of the elderly is usually a very important aspect of communication. Since they cannot see or hear as well, they must rely on physical contact for reassurance and a sense that the crisis worker is in control of the situation.
- Provide plenty of reassurance if it is necessary to transport an elderly person to a hospital, especially if their problem is relatively minor. Many elderly die in hospitals and nursing homes, and a trip to the hospital may be seen as their "last" trip if they are not reassured by the crisis worker.
- Treat an old person with respect. Call them by name and use their proper title. Involve them in decision making about their treatment.
- Be action oriented. Old people do not believe you are helping them if you only talk to them and do nothing.
- Provide accurate information to reduce their fears.
- Pay close attention to their physical complaints. Most of the time they are not just making them up to gain your attention.
- Be patient and take your time.
- Listen. It is common for old people to tell stories of their past life. This is not just a senile activity. Emotionally it is part of the aging process in which the person reviews their life and attempts to resolve old issues. Do not interrupt unless it is necessary.
- Be flexible and be prepared for changes in the person's condition.
- Clarify what you are doing to help them.
- Assure them that their care is confidential.
- Do not restrain them except as a last resort.
- Avoid medicating older people if possible.
- Allow family members or friends to stay with the crisis victim.

*Note:* The single reference (1) listed for aging in the reference section of this chapter is, by far, the most valuable reference that was discovered while researching this chapter.

161

## SUDDEN INFANT DEATH SYNDROME

## INTRODUCTION

The death of a child is a devastating loss for parents. When the death is sudden, its impact is even more intense and leaves parents in a state of shock and disbelief.

Crisis workers are typically deeply affected by such a loss and often find themselves confused about what to do or say to alleviate the intense emotional suffering of the parents. If they have children of their own, the management of the case is usually more difficult because of their emotional involvement.

This portion of the chapter will provide some useful guidelines that will assist crisis workers in combining compassion, tact, and an ability to function under great stress into an approach that will support parents in this most acute crisis.

## BACKGROUND

The Sudden Infant Death Syndrome is responsible for about 10,000 infant deaths a year. It is the greatest killer of children between the ages of one month and one year. The rate of occurrence is quite similar in most of the countries in the world.[2]

At present there is no known cause of the disease although several factors have been implicated. Sleep apnea (cessation of breathing for periods of time while sleeping), metabolic imbalances, brain dysfunction, abnormalities in cardiac electrical conduction, and respiratory tract infections are all being researched in an effort to solve the mystery of this disease.[2] Suffocation in bed clothes, vomiting, and choking are not usually involved in the death. SIDS (Sudden Infant Death Syndrome) is not considered hereditary. Neither is it contagious, and other children in the family are not necessarily at risk. In almost all cases, death by SIDS cannot be prevented. There are no warning signs and often the only symptom is death.[3]

Babies dying of SIDS die in their sleep and suffering and struggle are not part of the death process. The parents and other family members usually suffer intensely and may be considered the real "victims" of the syndrome.

162

Parents of babies who die of SIDS experience a "trauma grief" which is characterized by:

- Shock
- Denial
- Anger
- Depression
- Guilt
- Mental confusion
- Acute emotional vulnerability[4]

They are most in need of emotional support and accurate information.

## INTERVENTION SKILLS

Guidelines for the proper management of SIDS deaths are given below.

- If the baby is between one month and one year of age, suspect SIDS first before considering other diseases or abuse. (Deaths of children in this age range are only rarely caused by abuse. Children older than one year are not affected by SIDS.)
- Make every attempt to resuscitate the baby. This helps the parents to feel that everything possible was tried. But do not give the parents any false hope of success.
- Do not be overly silent. Parents can easily misinterpret silence and believe that it implies guilt.
- Do not accuse the parents of abuse, or, even worse, murder.
- Large "bruises" on the baby's body, bloody froth around the nose and mouth, and a distorted face are frequently present in SIDS cases. These signs should not be mistaken for child abuse.
- Gather information from the parents but do not judge or evaluate them. Do not tell them what they "should have" been doing before your arrival. Ask only the necessary

questions and do not invade the family's privacy. Too much questioning increases the parents' feelings of guilt and regret.

- Transport the infant to the hospital as soon as possible. Allow the parents to accompany their baby in the patient compartment of the ambulance.
- Do not allow them to drive themselves.
- Remind them to arrange for the care of other children in the family and to bring some money for phone calls, and other expenses.
- Listen carefully to their statements and questions and answer only with accurate information.
- Allow the parents to cry and express their sense of loss and hurt.
- Provide supportive care.
- If a police investigation of the death is underway, advise the parents that the investigation is routine and the questions you must ask do not imply fault on the part of the parents.
- In many states an autopsy is required in all sudden infant deaths. Some provision needs to be made to assure that the autopsy report is relayed to the parents as soon as possible.
- The key to successful management of a SIDS case is a supportive, compassionate, and tactful crisis worker who provides accurate information.

## DEATH AND DYING

Death which results from terminal illness brings with it a somewhat different set of emotional responses than the traumatic grief produced by SIDS. The slower approach to death gives both the dying person and his survivors a chance to resolve many emotional issues and prepare for the death in a less emotionally, disruptive manner.

### The Emotional Phases Of Terminal Illness

Elizabeth Kubler-Ross[7] worked with dying patients and discovered that practically all of them passed through a series of phases once they became fully aware that they were going to die. The phases are as follows:

- Denial
- Anger
- Bargaining
- Depression
- Acceptance

These phases are quite similar to the phases of crises described in Chapter One. It is suggested that the reader review Chapter One to obtain a fuller understanding of how these phases are interrelated.

Generally speaking, it takes a person a year or more to move through all of the phases. They do not necessarily occur in order and are frequently repeated before being fully resolved.

Feelings of isolation usually accompany most of the phases of dying. This is so because dying is something that people go through alone. They can be helped to some degree, but death is such an unknown thing that the living can only provide minimal help to the dying. This fact should not discourage crisis workers from being aware of the needs of the dying person and ready to provide whatever assistance they can.

## INTERVENTION SKILLS

- Become aware of your own fears and thoughts regarding death.
- Be ready to admit when a dying person reminds you of a loved one. If you are emotionally caught up in the helping process, you will be less able to help the dying person and his family. Once you admit that the person reminds you of somebody you care for, ask yourself if this person *is* your loved one. You will probably be able to say, "No, this person is not so and so. There is only a resemblance." You have now done what is called "reality testing." It usually frees a person up to work better in an emotionally charged situation. If working with a particular person is too distressing for you, get your partner or another member of the team to take over your role.
- Treat the dying person with respect and human warmth.

- Do not avoid them. They need your contact and they need you to talk with them.
- Dying people usually wish to discuss their situation. They are just afraid to do it for fear they will be rejected. Most often, they have things to say. They have certain preparations they wish to make financially and otherwise.
- Dying people are not upset by discussions of death as long as you do not take away all of their hope. Even in the very worst situations, they still need a bit of hope to hold onto.
- Touching a dying person is important. It helps them to maintain a sense of contact when their other senses are failing.
- Use words like "death." Do not substitute meaningless synonyms.
- Ask them how you might best help them. They can frequently guide you and make you feel somewhat more comfortable.
- Do not push them to talk. At times they prefer to be silent.
- Assist them in getting their family members together so they can give their final messages.
- Dying people, like the elderly, frequently feel it is necessary to review their lives. Allow them to talk. Show your interest and do not interrupt.
- Give factual information.
- Do not lie.
- Fulfill their requests as best as possible.
- Genuine warmth, understanding, and compassion will do more than anything else to assist a dying person.

*Note:* Elizabeth Kubler-Ross's work, *Death and Dying*[7] is a major resource. Crisis workers would do well to read the book. Most other references tend to repeat the major ideas expressed in this work.

## REFERENCES

1. Butler RN, Lewis MI: Aging and Mental Health, Positive Psychosocial Approaches, 2nd ed. St. Louis, C. V. Mosby Co., 1977
2. Public Health Service, Department of Health, Education and Welfare: "Facts about sudden infant death syndrome." Washington, DC; US

Government Printing Office, 1979

3. Staff Writer: "Evidence shows abnormalities before death in SIDS victims." US Medicine, March 1, 1977

4. Wanzenreid J: Sudden infant death syndrome parent. Brief publication distributed by the University of Nebraska. Omaha, Nebraska, Nebraska Sudden Infant Death Parents Group, date of publication not shown on document

5. Fulton R: SIDS: The survivor as victim. The Director, National Funeral Directors Association Publication, Vol. XLVI No. 10, October 1976

6. Weinstein S: SIDS, the role of the EMT. Emergency Product News, Vol. 9 No. 7, September 1977

7. Kubler-Ross E: On Death and Dying. New York, Macmillan Co., 1969

# CHAPTER 14

# *Multi-Casualty Situations*

Jeffrey T. Mitchell, M.S.

## INTRODUCTION

Multi-casualty crises produce a maximum of emotional distress in the shortest period of time. This is true for the victims and for the crisis workers. Major fires, transportation accidents, and natural disasters have the potential to kill or injure large numbers in a matter of seconds. Fire, police, rescue, and community resources (personnel, facilities, and equipment) may be quickly exhausted by the excessive demands of the situation. A period of confusion is likely to follow until the community is able to adjust to the new demands, or to receive intervention from resources outside of the community.

In a nation as large and as diversified as the US there is a potential every day for a man-made or natural disaster. The average emergency service worker experiences at least one multi-casualty incident in the course of his or her service.

The contents of this chapter will provide guidelines for the successful management of the emotional aspects of multi-casualty incidents.

## BACKGROUND

### Definition

Max Siporin, an author in the field of crisis intervention, defines a disaster as " . . . an extreme social crisis situation in which individuals and their social systems become dysfunctional and disorganized, sustain personal, collective, and public hardships, and also become a 'community of sufferers'."[1] In other words, it is a sudden, increased demand on the resources (fire, police, rescue, hospital, and government) of a particular community during a stressful period. In most disasters, there are numerous injuries, illnesses and/or deaths as well as serious psychological damage and the destruction of property. For the purposes of this chapter, five or more casualties of a serious nature will be considered a disaster.[2]

## Disaster Phases

Disasters usually have several fairly distinct, short and long-term phases. They are the heroic phase, honeymoon phase, disillusionment phase, and the reconstructive phase.

The *heroic phase* occurs immediately after the impact of the disasterous incident. People perceive the incident and begin to recognize the serious nature of the problem. They also make attempts to adapt to the incident.

The *honeymoon phase* occurs after people meet some success in adapting to the demands of the crisis. They are also pleased that they somehow survived the incident. There is a sense of closeness to fellow victims, who have shared the same dangers and have experienced the same problems.

The honeymoon phase eventually breaks down and the survivors experience disillusionment, anxiety, and depression. During the *disillusionment phase*, they become acutely aware of their losses and begin to feel isolated. Grief is a predominant reaction.

In the reconstructive phase, victims continue to grieve, but they make stronger efforts to re-establish their world. They rebuild, reorganize, seek outside help when their own resources fail, and they resolve their emotional and physical problems. [3,4]

Crisis workers usually see the victims during the heroic phase. This phase may be broken into several subphases. They are:

- Threat or warning period (not present in all disasters).
- Impact (the incident occurs).
- Inventory (the community quickly assesses the situation and checks its available resources).
- Rescue (the community resources are put into action).
- Remedy (the immediate priority needs of the crisis victims are worked on and resolved).[5]

# EMOTIONAL RESPONSES TO DISASTER

## A. The Victims

Surviving victims of a disaster experience similar emotional reactions to the phases of the crisis. During the threat phase, the victims feel anxious, apprehensive, and they tend to deny the reality of the situation. The impact phase produces tension, disorganization, disorientation, confusion, and feelings of agitation and hopelessness.

During the inventory phase, while the community is responding to the stresses of the crisis, the victims begin to feel apathetic, isolated, and depressed. They may also feel overwhelmed, angry, and extremely fearful. Denial and withdrawal from contact with others is also common. These feelings continue into the rescue phase and are supplemented by feelings of depression and regression (returning to less effective behaviors such as crying, hiding one's face, wringing of one's hands, and other signs).

It is not until the remedy phase that more positive emotions emerge. These emotions are usually associated with improved morale and a cooperative spirit, especially in light of the rescue efforts made by the community.[5, 6, 7]

It should be carefully noted that there is one emotional reaction that is usually *absent* during most disasters. That emotion is panic. Contrary to popular belief, only about ten percent of people involved in a disaster react with panic or total passivity. Most disaster victims react actively. They usually seek outside help only when they have exhausted their own resources. Panic usually only occurs when people feel trapped and faced with immediate danger from fire, explosion, flooding, or some other threat. A more typical reaction, after a brief, inactive, stunned period, is for people to "get together" and decide on leadership, and to respond to a leader's suggestion for concerted effort.[5, 8]

There are many long-term reactions to disasters. These emotional effects can last for several years. They are:

- Separation anxieties (fears of being abandoned by others which are very common among children).
- Insomnia (sleep disturbances).
- Nightmares.
- Disturbed memory.
- Withdrawal.

- Depression.
- Irritability.
- Phobias (irrational fears).
- Apprehension.
- Feelings of guilt and shame for having survived when others have perished, were injured, or lost their property.
- Feelings of resentment toward those who fared better than they.
- Increased smoking and drinking.
- Loss of appetites for sex and eating.
- Sexual impotence.
- Feelings of isolation.
- Deteriorating relationships with loved ones.
- Unresolved grief.
- Excessive concern over one's physical well-being.
- Feelings of hopelessness, helplessness, and a sense of meaninglessness to life.[6, 7, 9, 10]

Many of these long term reactions can be lessened or eliminated if emergency personnel respond efficiently to the emotional needs of crisis victims during the acute phases of the crisis (the first minutes and hours of a crisis).

## B. The Crisis Workers

Crisis workers also experience a set of emotional reactions to a disaster. These reactions are similar to the reactions experienced by the victims. They are:

- Confusion and disorganization.
- Anxiety.
- Apprehension.
- Feelings of helplessness and being overwhelmed.
- Frustration.
- Emotional callousness.
- Anger and irritability.
- Apathy.
- Loss of objectivity.[3, 5]
    (See Chaper 15 for information on burnout.)

## ASSESSMENT

The victims of disasters who experience many of the emotional reactions described in the preceding section usually can be classified under three main emotional categories: hysterical, subdued (or emotionally paralyzed by fear), and "adequately functioning."

## A. Hysterical

Victims of a multi-casualty incident are frequently hysterical. Hysteria is a state of emotional instability and extreme anxiety. It is characterized by agitation, screaming, weeping, fainting, and a general sense of panic and loss of control. There is frequently a sense of nausea, dizziness, tingling of the fingers and toes, mental confusion, and loss of muscle coordination. In extreme cases, there may be amnesia, extreme and irrational fears, paralysis of limbs (without injury to those parts), delirium, and convulsions.[11, 12, 13]

Hysterical individuals are dangerous at the scene of a disaster. They frequently run or wander into more danger, interfere with rescue efforts, become combative, and generally distract attention from more serious priorities. Hysterical behavior may mask serious underlying injuries in a victim. Another problem is that hysteria is spread to other victims who then begin to scream, panic, and produce more chaos.[14]

## Management of the Hysterical Person

A hysterical person can best be managed in one of the following ways:

1. Transport the person from the scene to a hospital immediately. Even if there is no evidence of injury, a hysterical person needs rapid medical (psychiatric) attention. The police may play a vital role in the control and transportation of a panicky victim. They should not underestimate their ability to help a hysterical person. If immediate transportation is not possible, the victim should at least be removed from the immediate scene.[14]

173

2. If transportation or removal from the immediate scene is impossible because of lack of adequate apparatus or personnel, the victim should be placed in the care of a responsible person who can provide support and care until the victim is transported. Other emergency service personnel or bystanders are often willing and able to fill this role.

3. In a situation in which transportation or individual care by a responsible person is not possible, the hysterical person can sometimes be calmed by direct, firm orders from a confident emergency service worker. The orders need to be simple, clear, and task oriented. "Stop moving.", "Hold this.", "I need your help . . . ", "Hold this pad on this man's arm.", "Don't let go until I tell you to.", "You are safe now. Just do what I say.", and "Come with me. I'll get someone to help you."

4. If no other method of managing a hysterical person is available, a sedative may be ordered by a physician and administered by a paramedic or nurse or an on-scene physician.

*Note:* NEVER slap or use any unnecessary or unusual force to control a panicky person. Slapping a victim usually only increases anxiety, agitation, and uncontrolled behavior. (There are also legal complications involved.) Calmness and control on the part of the crisis worker is the best treatment for a hysterical person. (See the section of this chapter on *General Techniques of Intervention in Disasters* for further details.)

## B. The Subdued Victim

The subdued victim is the most common in disaster incidents. The quiet victim of a disaster is often in more serious emotional difficulty than the loud, active hysterical person. An emotional storm is usually raging inside such a person. They are identified by their overall lack of activity and usually appear very subdued. They may sit and stare or wander about aimlessly. They are often paralyzed by fear, and the signs of shock are usually present. The person feels weak, dizzy, nauseous, and thirsty. Low blood pressure, a rapid and weak pulse, shallow respiration, shaking and trembling, profuse sweating and pale, moist skin may also be present. They are mentally confused and disoriented. Victims often feel numb or stunned. Their movements are random and uncoordinated.

## Management of the Subdued Person in Disasters

1. As in the treatment of the hysterical person, immediate transport from the scene is the treatment of choice. If this is not possible, removal from the immediate scene is essential. At the very least, the victim's view of the scene should be blocked by some object such as a blanket, rolled up and placed next to his head. See Figure 14.1.
2. Have the victim lie or sit down.
3. Treat for shock by keeping the victim warm, providing statements of reassurance, elevating the feet unless there is serious head or chest injury, and giving nothing by mouth.
4. Do not leave this victim alone. If emergency service personnel are too busy, a bystander may be called upon to help.
5. Do not sedate on the scene unless specifically ordered to do so by a physician.[15]

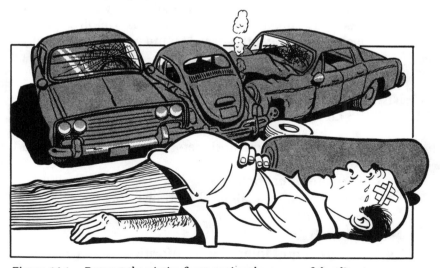

*Figure 14.1.   Prevent the victim from seeing the scene of the disaster.*

## C. The "Adequately Functioning" Victim

About one-fourth of the disaster victims will appear to be functioning adequately while at the scene. They will not be showing signs of either serious shock or hysteria. Some may even assist other victims or help rescue workers. Just because these victims do not appear to be emotionally distressed does not mean that they are fine. They are experiencing some emotional reactions and will eventually need help, although not as quickly as the hysterical or subdued victim. Crisis workers should not be fooled by these victims. Under continued stress, most of these victims will eventually break down and may then enter a state of emotional distress.

## Management Of the "Adequately Functioning" Victim

1. Relieve them of their rescue attempts as soon as reasonably possible, and remove them to an area where they may be checked for injuries and be provided with reassurance and basic care.
2. Transport these victims to medical facilities as soon as the more serious priority cases have been handled. Even if not obviously injured, they will need further evaluation and, possibly, some psychiatric intervention.
3. If they insist on continuing to help, assign them lighter tasks in the staging or treatment areas. Helping, in some cases, keeps the victim from "falling apart" emotionally.[6]

## GENERAL INTERVENTION TECHNIQUES APPLICABLE TO ALL TYPES OF MULTI-CASUALTY INCIDENTS

- Assess the situation and determine the needs for additional resources.
- Call in additional help.
- Prevent further casualties (a high priority).
- Rescue victims.
- Extinguish fires.
- Triage (sort out) injured into priorities and treat what is necessary.

176

- Evacuate the injured (by priority of injuries).
- Provide more elaborate treatment at hospital facilities.
- The command officer should establish a "Command Post," a triage area, a staging area, a temporary morgue, a family area, and a press section. (See suggestions in Figure 14.2.)
- Provide strong leadership (a central authority).
- Appoint an official spokesman to communicate with the press.
- Some official spokesman should be appointed to deal with family members who come to the scene to search for their relatives.
- Individuals and families seeking their relatives should be kept in one area, and should not be allowed to wander through the area where death and destruction is present.

## A. THE POLICE

- Police should set up road blocks, barricades, and check points to assure the security of the disaster scene.
- Uniforms, identification badges, or credentials are helpful at a disaster. They help the victims to gain a sense that someone is in control.
- Provide for traffic control. Keep access routes open.
- Provide crowd control.
- Keep the press away from victims and families searching for victims at the scene. This is done to prevent false reports or exaggerations from reaching the public and causing more chaos.
- Provide for information centers and rumor control in some instances.

## B. COMMUNITY RESOURCES

- Call clergymen to the scene. (These should be chosen from a pre-planned list.)
- Interpreters for deaf or foreign language victims may be necessary.
- Psychiatrists, psychologists, social workers, and coun-

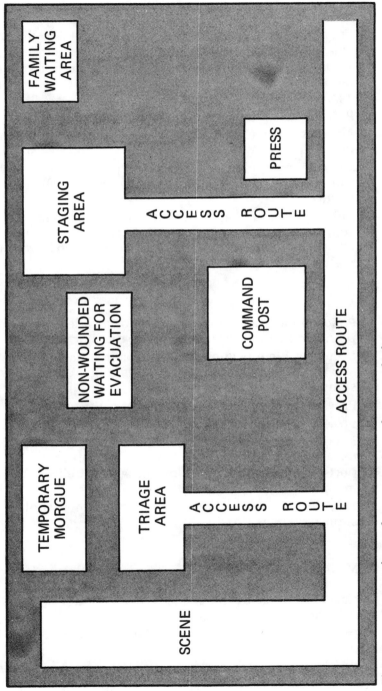

*Figure 14.2.   Suggested setup for an operation at the scene of a disaster.*

selors familiar with crisis intervention procedures should also be called to the scene and to hospitals receiving the injured. (Again, these professionals should be drawn from a pre-planned list.) These professionals not only provide emotional support; they frequently assist in the gathering of important information.

- Use "level headed" volunteers from among bystanders. They can be of great assistance if properly directed. They are especially helpful in dealing with victims of minor injuries.

## C. EMERGENCY MEDICAL SERVICE AND FIRE PERSONNEL

- Stay objective and set reasonable expectations. Total care of a victim at a disaster scene is impossible.
- Separate emotionally distressed victims from the rest to avoid spreading chaos.
- Reassure and provide accurate information to victims as you provide medical treatment.
- Provide for other needs such as food, clothing, blankets, coffee, and cots.
- Do not encourage any strange emotional behavior, but DO encourage the victims to talk about their experiences.
- Do not, however, allow victims to ramble on, especially if you need specific information. Interrupt them and ask another question.
- Keep patient information confidential from unauthorized people.
- Keep short, accurate records.
- Maintain good communications with the command post and provide accurate information.

## D. TRIAGE AND FAMILY AREAS

- Reunite families or groups as soon as possible.
- Encourage victims to accept certain tasks regarding their own care as soon as they are able.
- Provide shelter and privacy.
- Provide accurate, updated information.

179

- Avoid using sedatives and drugs.
- Do not make promises.
- Do not give false assurances.
- Be honest.
- Utilize people from the community to do jobs rather than outsiders whenever possible.
- Provide rest, food, and support to rescuers.
- If a body needs to be identified, someone should accompany family members to the morgue.

(Information provided in the intervention techniques section above was obtained from the following references: 2, 5, 14 through 23. Finally, follow-up emotional support will most likely be necessary for the victims and the rescuers involved in the incident. This should not be overlooked.)

## REFERENCES

1. Siporin M: Altruism, disaster, and crisis intervention. *In* Parad HJ et al (eds): Emergency and Disaster Management, A Mental Health Sourcebook. Bowie, MD; The Charles Press Publishers, Inc., 1976
2. Gann DS, Nagel E, Stafford JD, Walker F: Mass casualty management. *In* Zuidema G, Rutherford RB, Bollinger II WF (eds): Management of Trauma. Philadelphia, W. B. Saunders, 1979
3. Faberow NL, Frederick CJ: Training Manual for Human Service Workers in Major Disasters. Rockville, Maryland; US Department of Health, Education and Welfare, National Institute of Mental Health, DHEW publication No. (ADM) 77-538, 1978
4. Frederick CJ: Crisis intervention and emergency mental health. *In* Johnson WR (ed): Health in Action. New York; Holt, Rinehart and Winston, 1977
5. Kafrissen S, Heffran EF, Zusman J: Mental health problems in environmental disasters. *In* Resnik HLP, Ruben HL (eds): Emergency Psychiatric Care, The Management of Mental Health Crises. Bowie, Maryland, The Charles Press Publishers, Inc., 1975
6. Zusman J: Meeting mental health needs in a disaster: A public health view. *In* Parad HF et al (eds): Emergency and Disaster Management, A Mental Health Sourcebook. Bowie, Maryland; The Charles Press Publishers, Inc., 1976
7. Frederick CJ: Behavioral Aspects of Medical Emergencies in Disas-

ters. *In* Cowley RA (ed): Collected Papers in Emergency Medical Services and Traumatology. Baltimore, Institute for Emergency Medical Services, 1979

8. Dynes RR, Quarantelli EL: The family and community context of individual reactions to disaster. *In* Parad HF et al (eds): Emergency and Disaster Management, A Mental Health Sourcebook. Bowie, MD; The Charles Press Publishers, Inc., 1976

9. Schnaper N, Cowley RA: Voids in consciousness secondary to severe trauma. *In* Cowley RA (ed): Collected Papers in Emergency Medical Services and Traumatology. Baltimore, Maryland Institute for Emergency Medical Services, 1979

10. Titchener JL, Kapp FT: Family and character change at Buffalo Creek. American Journal of Psychiatry, 133:3, 295-299, March 1976

11. Wolman BB: Hysteria. *In* Wolman B et al (eds): Dictionary of Behavioral Science. New York, Van Nostrand Reinhold Company, 1973

12. Holsti OR: Crisis, stress and decision-making. International Social Science Journal, Vol. 23, 1971

13. Horowitz MF: Diagnosis and treatment of stress response syndromes, general principles. *In* Parad HF et al (eds): Emergency and Disaster Management. Bowie, MD; The Charles Press Publishers, Inc., 1976

14. Slaby AE, Lieb J, Tancredi LR: Handbook of Psychiatric Emergencies, A Guide for Emergencies in Psychiatry. New York, Medical Examination Publishing Company, Inc., 1975

15. Grant, H, Murray R: Emergency Care, 2nd edition. Bowie, MD; Robert J. Brady Co., 1978

16. Gazzaniga A, Iseri LT, Baren M (eds): Emergency Care: Principles and Practices for the EMT-Paramedic. Reston, VA; Reston Publishing Company, Inc., 1979

17. Vickery DM: Triage Problem-Oriented Sorting of Patients. Bowie, MD; Robert J. Brady Co., 1975

18. Popkin R: Role of the American Red Cross in maritime disasters. *In* Cowley RA (ed): Collected Papers in Emergency Medical Services and Traumatology. Baltimore, Maryland Institute for Emergency Medical Services, 1979

19. Dimick A: Role of medical staff in disaster planning and operations. *In* Cowley RA (ed): Collected Papers in Emergency Medical Services and Traumatology. Baltimore, Maryland Institute for Emergency Medical Services, 1979

20. Dynes RR: EMS delivery in disasters. *In* Cowley RA (ed): Collected Papers in Emergency Medical Services and Traumatology. Baltimore, Maryland Institute for Emergency Medical Services, 1979

21. Crowley L: The flight attendant as a first responder. *In* Cowley RA (ed): Collected Papers in Emergency Medical Services and Traumatology. Baltimore, Maryland Institute for Emergency Medical Services, 1979

22. Ingham RE: Transcultural consultation on crisis intervention. *In*

Parad HJ et al (eds): Emergency and Disaster Management, A Mental Health Sourcebook. Bowie, MD; The Charles Press Publishers, Inc., 1976

23. Hartsough DM, Zarle TH, Ottinger DR: Rapid response to disaster: The Monticello tornado. *In* Parad HF et al (eds); Emergency and Disaster Management, A Mental Health Sourcebook. Bowie, MD; The Charles Press Publishers, Inc., 1976

# CHAPTER **15**

# Crisis Worker Stress and Burn Out

Jeffrey T. Mitchell, M.S.

## INTRODUCTION

This chapter has been written for each of you—the administrators, the police officers, the fire-rescue, emergency medical personnel, and others who have read this book with the idea of helping people. Hopefully, this chapter will provide guidelines for dealing with yourselves. In helping others, there is a price to be paid. Each distressing case puts a tiny dent in your psyche and, over time, your own condition becomes vulnerable to deterioration and the initiation of personal crises. This chapter can help you to recognize some danger signals and to do something before too much damage is done to your bodies and to your lives. It is sincerely hoped that there is still time to repair the damages that have occurred already and to prevent further deterioration.

## BACKGROUND

Every year there is an enormous turnover in police, fire, emergency medical, rescue, and other crisis worker positions. (Volunteer and auxiliary emergency service personnel are not exceptions to the turnover rule.) Besides the turnover in personnel, there is much more illness recorded among crisis workers than among workers in other types of employment. A high attrition rate and illness are not coming out of the blue sky. There is a reason, and it is commonly called "burn out." Burn out is the final step in a process of straining a person over an extended period of time. The stress produces a number of physiological, pychological, cognitive, and behavioral changes in the person.[3] These changes will be discussed at greater length later in this chapter.

It is important to clarify a few definitions so everyone will have the same basis from which to work when considering stress and burn out. First, it is important to note that stress is not all bad. It is the common characteristic of all biological activity.[4] Generally speaking, it is stress that produces human progress. If people were totally happy with things as they are, no one would invent, create, move around, explore, or attempt to change.[5] Stress is not nervous tension, and it is not something to be totally eliminated. It has a very healthy side to it. There is some optimum level of stress which produces growth. Beyond that, it is damaging and could be called "distress."[3,6,7]

Stress is simply the force placed against an object or a person and the psychological and physical response of the person to the force. Stress always produces some strain or distortion in the object or person being stressed. Mild stress produces little strain, while moderate stress produces greater strain, and severe stress generates a very great strain and may produce a collapse of the object or person.[8]

Stress is associated with the words "stressor" and "strain." The stressor is the actual event. The event produces a demand (stress) upon the person to adapt or respond to the stressor. Adaptation uses up some energy and fatigues the person to some degree. The wear and tear on the person is called strain. This is diagramed below.

| Stressor (event) | → Stress | → Strain |
|---|---|---|
| Call for adaptation | Psychological and physiological response of the person | wear and tear on the person |

Hans Selye, one of the most famous researchers in the field of stress, proposed the above understanding of stress in the late 1930s. He calls stress a "nonspecific" response of the body to any demand.[9] It is nonspecific because the same physiological and psychological reactions occur regardless of the stressor (fear, excitement, anxiety, and others). He stated that stress is not so much the event, but the perception of the event by the person. An event is perceived as a stressful one if it is viewed as harmful, or if the person's coping mechanisms are thought to be inadequate.[9,10]

The concept of stress is not a new one. It has been around for thousands of years. Epictetus, the ancient Greek philosopher once said, "People are disturbed not by things, but by the views they take of them." About one hundred years ago, a physician by the name of Daniel Hock Tuke wrote a book entitled, *Illustrations of the Influence of the Mind on the Body* which discussed the occurrence of disease in people subjected to great stress.[11]

It was not until Hans Selye performed his physiological studies in the thirties, that scientific evidence was gathered to demonstrate the harmful effects of excessive stress on the human body and mind.[9]

There are three major categories of stress:

A. Frustration
B. Conflict
C. Pressure.

Any stressful event will fall under one of these three categories. Constant change is a major source of stress. Some others are delays, failure, losses, death, financial problems, social disapproval, guilt, and illness.[8] This list is by no means complete.

## THE GENERAL STRESS REACTION

As noted in the background section of this chapter, there are physical and psychological reactions to events which are perceived as stressful. The reaction is generalized to most animal life and has been named the "General Adaptation Syndrome" by Hans Selye.[9]

The stress reaction in humans and most animals is defensive in nature. It is generally aimed at survival. We often speak of it as a "flight or fight" response. Adrenalin gets pumped into the blood along with a higher level of blood glucose. Blood pressure and heart rate rise and the respiratory rate increases and deepens. Muscle tone is enhanced and the organism is ready to run or attack. There is also an enhancement of the clotting mechanisms in the blood. The person usually has accompanying psychological reactions such as fear, anxiety, and anger among others. There is a general response regardless of whether the event is fear producing, anger-producing, or anxiety-producing.[3,9,12,13] (More recent research, however, is pointing out that the body does provide different biochemical reactions for different stimuli.[12] For the purposes of this chapter, however, it is helpful to recognize and deal with just the general nature of the human response to stress.)

The general adaptation syndrome or standard psychological and physical response to the stressful events can become harmful to the body under certain conditions. *Prolonged exposure to stress almost always produces psychological and physical damage.* [5] It is believed that excessive, prolonged stress inhibits the immune systems in the body and leaves a person vulnerable to diseases including heart disease and cancer. [5]

## ASSESSING THE STRESS

Remember that each person is unique and each can tolerate a different level of stress. There are a number of factors that need to be considered when looking at stress.

First, the *degree* of stress is important. As stated earlier, a mild degree of stress produces little or no strain, but a severe stress produces severe strain. Next, the *duration* of stress must be considered. Even severe stress may be tolerated well if it is short in duration. The *number* of stresses occurring at the same time or within a fairly close time frame is also important. Many stresses over a reasonably brief period of time, or happening at the same time, may raise the overall degree of stress to a damaging level. [14]

*Psychological stress* such as death of a spouse or the break up of a love relationship is considered more damaging than *physiological stress* such as a broken bone or a case of pneumonia. [15] Stress also becomes much more severe if a person views it as *life or limb threatening* or *threatening to one's general well-being*, so *perception of the stress, is important.* [8,10,12]

Two other factors need to be taken into account when evaluating the level of one's stress. The first is the *level of previous experiences.* If a person has had a good record of adapting successfully under stress in the past, he or she has a better chance of adapting to a current stress. A person has a better chance of handling stress if he or she has a *set of reliable resources* such as a supportive family and a large circle of friends. [8]

## MEASURING YOUR OWN STRESS

The Holmes stress scale [15] has been included for your evaluation of your individual stress. Make a note of the items on the scale that have occurred in your life during the last calendar year and add up the total number of points. Please note that good events cause stress too. Any time people have to adapt, stress is produced. Do this now and then continue to read on.

---

### *STRESS SCALE*

---

| | |
|---|---:|
| Death of a spouse | 100 |
| Divorce | 73 |
| Marital separation | 65 |
| Detention in jail | 63 |
| Personal injury or illness | 53 |
| Marriage | 50 |
| Being fired from work | 47 |
| Being retired from work | 45 |
| Marital reconciliation | 45 |
| Change in health or behavior of family member | 44 |
| Pregnancy | 40 |
| Major business readjustment | 39 |
| Sexual difficulties | 39 |
| Change in financial status | 38 |
| Death of a close friend | 37 |
| Change in line of work | 36 |
| Change in number of arguments with spouse | 35 |
| Mortgage or loan greater than $10,000 | 31 |
| Foreclosure of mortgage or loan | 30 |
| Gaining a new family member | 30 |
| Son or daughter leaving home | 29 |
| Change in responsibilities at work | 29 |
| In-law troubles | 29 |
| Outstanding personal achievement | 28 |
| Wife beginning, or ceasing, work | 26 |
| Change in living conditions | 25 |
| Beginning or ceasing formal school | 26 |
| Change in personal habits | 24 |
| Troubles with boss | 23 |
| Change in residence | 20 |
| Change in working hours or conditions | 20 |
| Changing to a new school | 20 |
| Change in recreational habits | 19 |
| Change in church activities | 19 |
| Mortgage or loan less than $10,000 | 17 |
| Change in sleeping habits | 16 |
| Change in eating habits | 15 |

| | |
|---|---|
| Change in family get togethers | 15 |
| Christmas | 12 |
| Minor violations of the law | 11 |

Used with permission. Holmes T, Rahe RH: The social readjustment rating scale. Journal of Psychosomatic Research 11, 1967, pp. 213-218.

You start off with a ten percent chance of going into a hospital within a two year period regardless of your stress level. If you scored less than 150, you are probably handling your stress reasonably well. If you scored between 150 and 200, your vulnerability for a serious illness within a two year period increases to approximately 50 percent. If you scored over 300 points, your chances rise to 90 percent.[15] A serious illness is defined as one which requires about four trips to a doctor and keeps a person feeling sick for about a week.[16]

## BURN OUT

Besides making you vulnerable to a variety of illnesses, prolonged and acute stress can produce a syndrome called "burn out." Burn out is a descriptive word which implies the loss of an energy source and the useless remains of a once functional system. As described in the background section of this chapter, "burn out" is a final step faced by a person exposed to a high level of stress.[17,18,19] There are two types of burn out, rapid onset and gradual burn out, resulting from prolonged exposure to stress.

## RAPID ONSET BURN OUT

Rapid onset burn out is usually developed when people are exposed to overwhelming stress for even relatively short periods of time. It occurs when the emergency service worker has used most or all of his effective energy and is still not able to cope adequately with the situation.[21] Typical examples of stressful events which might tax the coping abilities of the crisis worker are mass casualty, natural or man made disasters, and volatile hostage incidents. Individuals who experience rapid onset burn out have actually reached a state of severe exhaustion and it is not likely that continued activity at the scene will be effective. In fact, it may be dangerous to themselves and to the people they are trying to assist.[22] Therefore, field supervisory personnel should be aware of the following symptoms and should be ready to relieve their personnel if the symptoms appear. Early recognition is the key to successful alleviation of the burn out problem. If the emergency service worker is given a short rest period before the symptoms become too severe, he should be able to return to the scene and function effectively.

| *Symptoms of Rapid Onset Burn Out* | |
| --- | --- |
| Psychological | • A high level of anxiety<br>• Increased irritability<br>• Feelings of depression<br>• Inability to control emotions<br>• Increased excitability<br>• Feelings of apathy<br>• Feelings of isolation[2] |
| Physical | • Severe fatigue<br>• Tremors<br>• Headaches<br>• Gastrointestinal upset<br>• Excessive sweating<br>• Chills<br>• Symptoms of shock[5] |
| Thought | • Poor concentration<br>• Indecisiveness<br>• Confusion in thought<br>• Slow thinking<br>• Loss of objectivity<br>• Inability to express clear thoughts<br>• Forgetfulness[5,20,21] |

## INTERVENTION SUGGESTIONS FOR RAPID ONSET BURN OUT

- Be aware of the symptoms and intervene early if they appear.
- Ask the individual to take a break.
- Order him to take a break if asking fails.
- Point out that his ability to function effectively is lessened because of his fatigue.
- Allow the worker to return to the scene if he takes the rest period and improves.
- Provide food.

189

- Provide beverages such as milk, coffee, tea, or soft drinks.
- Provide lavoratory facilities.
- Provide a place to sit down or lie down away from the scene and out of sight of the scene.
- Provide blankets, dry clothes, or other needs. Allow him to talk about the situation, express his anger, frustration, and other emotions.
- Allow him to have some quiet time alone.
- Remove him from the scene if the symptoms seem excessive.

## GRADUAL BURN OUT

Gradual burn out takes months and sometimes years to develop to a point where the individual can no longer be effective in a job and must therefore resign his position. There are plenty of warning signs which occur along the way. If attention is paid to the warning signals early enough, the burn out can be reversed.[21] A gradual burn out has much more serious and permanent effects than a rapid onset type, and it is generally more difficult to cure.

Gradual burn out seems to develop in four, more or less, distinct stages. *The symptoms of the earlier stages are included in each more serious stage.* (The following stages of burn out have been developed from the author's readings, clinical experience, and intuition, not from statistical research.)

### Stage I—The Early Warning Signs.

- Vague anxiety
- Constant fatigue
- Feelings of depression
- Boredom with one's job
- Apathy

### Stage II—Initial Burn Out.

- Lowered emotional control
- Increasing anxiety

190

- Sleep disturbances
- Headaches
- Diffuse back and muscle aches
- Loss of energy
- Hyperactivity
- Excessive fatigue
- Moderate withdrawal from social contact
- Nausea[2,3,5]

## Stage III—Burn Out.

- Skin rashes
- Generalized physical weakness
- Strong feelings of depression
- Increased alcohol intake
- Increased smoking
- High blood pressure
- Migraine headaches
- Loss of appetite for eating
- Loss of sexual appetite
- Ulcers
- Severe withdrawal
- Excessive irritability
- Emotional outbursts
- Development of irrational fears (phobias)[5,12]
- Inflexibility in thought

## Stage IV—Burn Out.

- Asthma
- Coronary artery disease
- Diabetes
- Cancer
- Heart attacks
- Severe depression
- Lowered self esteem
- Inability to function in job or personal affairs
- Severe withdrawal
- Uncontrolled crying spells

- Suicidal thoughts
- Muscle tremors
- Severe fatigue
- Over-reaction to emotional stimuli
- Agitation
- Constant tension
- Accident proneness
- Carelessness
- Feelings of hostility
- Development of moderate to severe thought disorders [5,11,12,20]

## COPING WITH STRESS

The following list of guidelines will be useful in helping emergency service personnel to reduce their stress and its negative effects. The list is not all inclusive and many other things can be done. Recognize the fact that you *do* have options and that you can change yourself or things in your environment.[10] You can do this by:

A. *Changing the environment:*
Cutting down on noise, improving lighting, providing an adequate work space, cutting down on crowding, eliminating dirt, providing adequate ventilation, and using protective devices.

B. *Changing yourself through:*
training, learning more, and building up your current resources.

C. *Reducing the harmful effects of stress.*
If changing the environment and changing yourself are not possible, reduce the harmful effects of stress by:
Seeking out medical treatment
Involving yourself in counseling
Widening your circle of friends
Being firm about your rights and needs to superiors.[12]

Also:

- Do your best to think logically. Shut down the overactive emotional responses.
- Eat well balanced meals.

- Use vitamins B and C. (They are especially helpful to the body in periods of stress.)[12]
- Keep up healthy physical activities.
- Take breaks.
- Increase leisure time.
- Increase social activity.
- Meditate if you like.
- Recreation. *Play hard and play often.*
- Decrease your work load.
- Clarify the number and degree of your responsibilities.
- Match your skills with the job to be performed.
- Relax often. Use relaxation exercises and yoga, if you like.[5,12,14,23]
- Meet with colleagues and discuss problems on a regular basis.
- Talk to your leaders and bosses.
- Accept psychotherapy or other types of help if you are in the advanced stages of burn out. You usually cannot get out on your own. You and your family will suffer if you delay too long.
- Establish a group that meets specifically to work on the expression and handling of feelings of anger, grief, frustration, and isolation that arise in the crisis worker. Knowing that others feel the way you do can help you to cope better with your own feelings.
- Set up a list of priorities and get the essentials done. Do not be overly concerned about items near the end of the list.
- Do activities that will have a high probability of success.
- Take vacation time.
- Be flexible and be ready to change directions.
- Get plenty of rest.
- Use your power to fantasize (daydream).
- Look at the long term goals. It helps to keep the present in perspective.
- Never choose from just two alternatives. Always devise three or more from which to choose.
- Do not be afraid to admit you are in real trouble.
- Stay off drugs unless you are using them according to a physician's prescription.
- Alcohol is not a substitute for real help. It usually complicates and prolongs the problem.
- Get involved in activities that have little or nothing to do with emergency services, but which provide a sense of

personal satisfaction.
- Share your distress with the people you love. They can be a big support.

These references were most helpful in devising the above suggestions:[5,8,10,12, and 18].

## REFERENCES

1. Dutton LM, Smolensky MH, Lorinor R et al: Psychological stress levels in paramedics. Emergency Medical Services, September/October 1978
2. Sedgwick R: Psychological responses to stress. Journal of Psychiatric Nursing and Mental Health Services, September/October 1975
3. Selye H: Stress and distress. Comprehensive Therapy, Vol. 1 No. 8, December 1976
4. Roberts S: Stress. Behavioral Concepts and Nursing Throughout the Life Span. Englewood Cliffs, NJ; Prentice-Hall, Inc., 1978
5. Pelletier KR: Mind As Healer, Mind As Slayer, A Holistic Approach to Preventing Stress Disorders. New York, Delta Publishing Co., 1977
6. Oken D: Stress . . . Our Friend, Our Foe. In Stress: A Blue Print for Health. Vol. 25 No. 1, Chicago, Blue Cross Association, 1974
7. Ward B: Stress may not be hazardous to your health. Sky, March 1979
8. Coleman C: Psychology and Effective Behavior. Glenview, IL; Scott, Foresman and Co., 1969.
9. Selye H: The evolution of the stress concept. American Scientist, November/December 1973
10. Willis RW: Options in managing stress. Pediatric Nursing, January/February 1979
11. Weiss JM: Psychological factors in stress and disease. Scientific American, June 1972
12. Cox T: Stress. Baltimore, University Park Press, 1978
13. Herbert DJ: Psychophysiological reactions as a function of life stress and behavioral rigidity. Journal of Psychiatric Nursing and Mental Health Services, Vol. 14, 23-27, May 1976
14. Lazarus RS: Psychological Stress and the Coping Process. New York, McGraw-Hill, 1966
15. Holmes TH, Rahe RH: The social readjustment rating scale. Journal of Psychosomatic Research 11 (1967): 213-218

16. Holmes TH, Holmes TH: How change can make us ill. *In* Blue Print for Health, prepared by the Blue Cross Association, Chicago, 1974
17. Kobren G: Nurse Burnout. The Sun Magazine (Baltimore Sun Papers) October 7, 1979
18. Hall RC, Gardner ER, et al: The professional burnout syndrome. Psychiatric Opinion, Vol. 16 No. 4, April 1979
19. Maslach C, Jackson SE: Burn-out cops and their families. Psychology Today, May 1979
20. Farberow NL, Frederick CJ: The burn out syndrome. Training Manual for Human Service Workers in Major Disasters, Washington, DC; US Government Printing Office, 1978
21. Farberow NL, Frederick CJ: Disaster relief workers' burn-out syndrome. Field Manual for Human Service Workers in Major Disasters. Washington, DC; US Government Printing Office, 1978
22. Journal S: The Transparent Self. New York, Van Nostrand Reinhold Company, 1971
23. Singer J, Glass DC: Making your world more livable. Stress, Chicago, Blue Cross Association, 1974

# Rapid Reference

## Jeffrey T. Mitchell, M.S.

The Rapid Reference Section contains only a summary of the more important guidelines which should be followed when working with specific crises under field conditions. For background information and more detailed guidelines, the reader should refer to the material contained within the main body of this book. Many of the techniques are useless without familiarity with the concepts described within the text.

### AGED IN CRISIS

**Interventions:**

- Do not joke or unnecessarily discuss old people's appearance with them.
- Be respectful.
- Do not treat old people like children.
- Do not mistake hearing or sight difficulties for intellectual inferiority.
- Old people find it hard to ask for help. Do not belittle them if they do ask for help.
- Evaluate the crisis in light of the person's history.
- Touching is very important. The aged depend more on touch since sight and hearing may not be adequate.
- Be reassuring.
- Be action oriented.
- Be patient.
- Listen carefully to old people and try to fulfill their requests if they are within reason.
- Do not restrain if it can be avoided.
- Allow family members to accompany the victim.

## ALCOHOL EMERGENCIES

Alcohol intoxication can be:

    A. Mild—needs no special treatment.
    B. Acute—may or may not need special treatment.
    C. Complicated—almost always demands special treatment in a hospital. (Examples are violence, suicide, other drugs, medical problems.)

Withdrawal from alcohol can consist of:

    A. Tremors.
    B. Hallucinations.
    C. Combination of A and B.
    D. Convulsions.
       (All of the above need special hospital treatment.)

Assessment is done by:

    A. Looking first.
    B. Talking and listening second.
    C. Touching third.

DO NOT:

    A. Rush.
    B. Joke about, ridicule, or judge the person.
    C. Shine your light in their eyes.
    D. Work alone.
    E. Argue.
    F. Make sudden movements.
    G. Make loud noises.
    H. Leave the patient alone.
    I. Give any more alcohol.
    J. Lie to the person.
    K. Put in a brightly lit or shadowed room.
    L. Let antagonizing stimuli like crowds get near the person.
    M. Use restraints if you can avoid them.

DO:

    A. Take suicidal and homicidal risks seriously.
    B. Call for additional help if necessary.
    C. Keep calm.
    D. Treat medically if necessary.
    E. Treat the person with respect.
    F. Notify the receiving hospital.
    G. Talk to the person.
    H. Protect yourself.
    I.  Give food, candy, or non-alcoholic beverages.
    J.  Take a good history.
    K. Get a family member of friend to help.

## BURN OUT

### Rapid Onset Burn Out—At the Scene

Symptoms:

| | |
|---|---|
| Psychological | Increased anxiety |
| | Increased irritability |
| | Feelings of acute depression |
| | Poor emotional control |
| | Increased excitability |
| | Feelings of apathy |
| | Feelings of isolation |
| Physical | Severe fatigue |
| | Tremors |
| | Headaches |
| | Nausea |
| | Gastrointestinal upset |
| | Excessive sweating |
| | Chills |
| | Symptoms of shock |
| Thought | Poor concentration |
| | Indecisiveness |
| | Confusion in thought |
| | Slow thinking |
| | Loss of objectivity |
| | Inability to express clear thoughts |
| | Forgetfulness |

## Intervention Techniques

- Be aware of the symptoms
- Intervene early
- Ask the individual to take a break
- Order him if necessary
- Point out his lowered ability to function
- Provide food
- Provide non-alcoholic beverages
- Provide bathroom facilities
- Provide quiet place to sit down or lay down
- Provide blankets
- Provide dry clothing
- Allow person to talk about his experience or to express his emotions
- Remove the individual from the scene entirely if symptoms persist
- Allow him to return to duties if he improves

## CHILD ABUSE AND NEGLECT

- Child abuse is always considered whenever a child is injured and the cause of the injury is not known.
- Approach child slowly
- Look first, talk second, and touch third
- Be gentle
- Get on the same eyeball level with the child
- Note:
  - Bruises, burns, and other marks
  - Inappropriate dress
  - If child is excessively frightened
  - If child withdraws
  - If child is possibly too affectionate
  - If child and surroundings are dirty
  - No supervision of child
  - Old injuries
  - History of previous run to same house
  - Evidence of malnutrition such as swelled stomach, wasted buttocks

## CHILD ABUSE AND NEGLECT (CONTINUED)

### Interviewing Child and Parents

- Children will try to protect parents
- Do not make accusations
- Do not make judgments
- Do not interrogate
- Ask questions that are pertinent to current problem

### Intervention

- Assure safety of child
- Transport to hospital
- If parents object, police should be called in
- Do not express anger to parents
- Be as compassionate as possible
- Do not photograph unless you are responsible for evidence
- Do not undress child completely. If undressing is necessary, leave underpants on
- Assign female staff to case if possible
- Document for records all factual information
- Report all information and suspicions to hospital staff or police
- Refer parents to social agencies whenever possible
- Do not confuse sudden infant death syndrome with child abuse. If in doubt treat as a sudden infant death

## CHILDHOOD CRISES

- Separation from parents, especially the mother, produces the greatest anxiety for children.

### Interventions:

- Remove the child from the immediate scene
- Do not leave the child alone

- Talk to the child
- Call him by name
- Use simple language
- Be honest
- Tell him what you are going to do before you do it
- Do not threaten the child if he does not cooperate with your efforts to help
- Allow the child to cry or otherwise express his emotions. Do not tell him things like, "Big boys don't cry."
- Do not criticize the child's family or living conditions in his presence

# COMMUNICATIONS

## Communications Summary

**Be:**

- Honest
- Warm
- Caring
- Empathetic

Use if appropriate:

- Eye contact
- Touching
- Offer food, clothing, blankets, or other articles
- Calm, even voice tones
- Patience (do not rush)

# CRISIS INTERVENTION

- A crisis is a state of emotional turmoil.

Crises are:

- Sudden
- Not prepared for
- Short in duration
- Potentially dangerous

Victims respond with:

- High anxiety
- Denial
- Anger
- Remorse (sadness and guilt)
- Grief

Crisis intervention:

- Temporary but active entry into the situation

Goals:

- Protect victim
- Mobilize resources
- Get victim functioning again

## Crisis Intervention Format

1. Assess
2. Plan
3. Implement plan
4. Check the plan
5. Recap events with the victim

## General Crisis Intervention Techniques

- Take your time unless a medical emergency is present
- Be calm
- Remove victim from harmful environment
- Reassure the victim
- Talk to the victim
- Touch appropriately
- Direct crisis victims to perform specific tasks
- Take some action to resolve the problem
- Show confidence

- Allow the victim to express emotions
- Listen carefully
- Be compassionate and understanding
- Tell the truth. (It is not necessary to tell the victim everything if it is potentially upsetting.)
- Do not argue with the victim
- Do not take the victim's emotions personally

## I. ASSESSMENT

Goal: Answer these questions:
Who, What, When, Where, Why

Method:

A. Interview
- Introduce yourself
- State the purpose of the interview
- Scan the environment for hidden dangers
- Organize crisis scene
- Gather information
- Close interview

B. Diagnosis (or judgment about information)
- Whether situation is chronic or acute?
- Life or limb threatening?
- Psychologically threatening?
- Situation:
  1. Severe
  2. Moderate
  3. Mild
- Is victim coping adequately?
- What resources are available for help?
- Other factors?

## II. PLAN—NEEDS TO BE:

- Short term
- Practical
- Immediate
- Action oriented
- Organized
- Within capabilities and limitations of crisis worker
- Made with victim's involvement
- A provision for referral to another source of help

## III. ACTION

- Get the plan operating

## DEATH AND DYING

### Interventions:

- Be respectful to the dying person and the family members
- Do not interrupt a dying person who is telling their story unless it is necessary for their care
- Dying people usually wish to discuss their situation
- Do not take away all of their hope
- Touching of the victim is important since their senses are failing
- Give factual information
- Fulfill requests as best as possible
- Provide reassurance and support to the survivors
- Depending on the circumstances, referrals to helping agencies might be necessary

You may find a victim in one of the following phases in the dying process:
- Denial
- Anger
- Bargaining
- Depression
- Acceptance

205

## Interventions:

- Remove young children from the immediate scene.
- Interview participants in the crisis separately.
- Do not take sides.
- Be calm.
- Be careful. Families are highly volatile when in a state of emotional crisis. They can hurt the crisis workers.
- Do not touch family members during periods of high tension. It might be interpreted as an attack.
- Try to get at least one family member to cooperate with you in your intervention plan.
- Use restraints sparingly.
- Refer the family to a counseling center or a professional where they can receive help in resolving their problems.

### DISASTER

## Interventions:

- Remove hysterical people from the scene immediately.
- Never slap a panicky person. It usually makes them worse.
- Have an emotionally shocked victim lie or sit down.
- Treat emotionally depressed victims for shock.
- Do not sedate at the scene unless specifically ordered to do so by a responsible physician.
- Do not let survivors help too much in the rescue efforts.
- Appoint official spokesmen for dealing with the press and families of the victims.
- Wearing of uniforms and the display of identification helps to keep the confusion down.
- Stay objective.
- Reassure the victims.
- Provide food, blankets, clothing, and other aids.
- Keep patient information confidential.
- Reunite families or groups as soon as possible.

## FAMILY CRISES

The ACTION plan for families in crisis:
    A—Assess the situation.
    C—Control the problem. Be in command.
    T—Treat according to the priorities.
    I—Inform the family members of important information.
    O—"Okay" or encourage and support the family.
    N—Notate or keep good records.

## LEGAL MATTERS IN CRISIS

In most states, emergency service personnel are protected from liability by the "Good Samaritan Laws." If you do what is prudent and reasonable, and act according to established standards, your chances of being sued are minimal.

- Do not violate a person's rights to privacy.
- Do not violate a person's basic civil rights by unnecessarily restraining or confining that person.
- Do not touch a person without that person's consent unless a mitigating emergency circumstance exists.
- Never use excessive force to control a combative crisis victim.
- Use the proper equipment to restrain a person.
- Do not leave the person unattended once you have begun your intervention.
- A person has the right to refuse care as long as he is over 18 (in most states), in control of his behavior and mental faculties, and is not dangerous to himself or others.
- If you are in doubt, act in favor of performing the treatment.
- Keep accurate records.
- Keep victim records confidential.
- Report those incidents dictated by local laws to the proper authorities.
- Try to obtain a signed release from a person who refuses care.

## MENTAL (EMOTIONAL) DISTURBANCES

The majority of severely mentally disturbed people are *NOT* dangerous to themselves or to others.

Symptoms:

Anxiety
Depression
Unreasonable fears
Disorganized thinking
Hallucinations              } Indicate more
Emotional extremes            serious disturbances
Physical uncoordination

Interventions:
- Remove annoying stimuli from the environment.
- Let the person know that you want to help.
- Respond with understanding to the person's comments.
- Focus on the immediate problem.
- Offer alternatives to the person's behavior.
- Advise the person of what you are going to do.
- Do not lie to an emotionally disturbed person.
- Do not display weapons unless it is absolutely necessary.
- Do not agree or disagree with the person's false perceptions.
- Do not argue with the person.
- Restrain only as a last resort.
- Do not make any promises that you might not be able to keep.
- Move slowly and cautiously when dealing with a disturbed person.
- Talk in calm, even tones which imply control, confidence, and interest in the person.
- Do not joke with or ridicule the person.
- Treat the person with respect.

## SEXUAL ASSAULT

Rape, as all forms of sexual assault, is not a crime of passion or sexuality. It is life threatening violence. The initial reaction of most victims is terror and extreme fear for life. Rape victims do not have to report the crime and confidentiality is vital in rape cases.

## I. Assessment Tasks

- Believe that the victim is telling truth.
- Check the need for:
  Medical treatment.
  Special support units (canine, helicopter, ambulance, crime lab, sexual offense investigation unit, or others).
  Preserving evidence.
- Check victim's emotional state (calm, hysterical, withdrawn, or other emotions).

## II. Intervention Tasks

- Be calm and confident.
- Listen carefully.
- Do not touch the victim except to administer first aid.
- Get the suspect's description broadcast.
- Talk to the victim as much as possible. Tell her what is going on.
- Transport victim to the hospital if necessary.
- Advise victim not to douche, bathe, change clothes, urinate, defecate, eat, or drink.
- Do not undress victim.
- Do not examine genital area.
- Do not leave her alone.
- Do not joke or talk about irrelevant topics.
- Do not ask her details about the rape.
- Fulfill victim's primary needs.
- Secure the crime scene.
- Make victim comfortable.
- Reduce activity around victim.
- Reassure victim that she is safe.
- Ask victim's permission before taking actions that directly affect her.
- Perform careful, in-depth formal interview.
- Gather statements from any witnesses.
- Gather all evidence.

- Maintain constant chain of custody of evidence.
- Make proper referrals to the victim of the places that can continue to help her.

## Child Victims

- Assure their safety and physical well-being.
- Imply no guilt.
- Do not focus *too* much attention on them. This could produce feelings of guilt.
- Recommend psychiatric consultation for parents.

### SUBSTANCE ABUSE

## Questions for Assessment:

- Type
- Dose or amount
- How taken
- When taken
- Observations about the victim
- Level of consciousness
- Behavior
- Overall medical conditions

## Treatment:

- Treat medical problems symptomatically
- Stay calm and confident
- Reduce stimuli
- Reassure the victim
- Watch for changes
- Do not argue
- Use victim's friends to help him
- Keep victim in contact with reality
- Take your time
- Only one person does the talking
- Touch if appropriate
- Provide food and non-alcoholic drinks

- Move slowly
- Do not work alone
- Do not leave the victim alone
- Shut off flashing lights
- Do not use siren
- Avoid restraints unless necessary
- Keep restraints on once you use them

## Talk Down:

- Use a soft, calm voice
- Reassure the victim that he is safe and not going crazy
- Suggest pleasant places, people, and things to the victim
- Provide support, care, empathy, and warmth
- Suggest peace, quiet, and safety continuously

### SUDDEN INFANT DEATH SYNDROME

Children older than one year are usually not affected by SIDS. Interventions:

- Make every effort to resuscitate the infant.
- Do not accuse the parents of abuse or neglect.
- Do not be overly silent. That may imply guilt to the parents.
- Do not mistake large bruise-like blotches on the baby's body for signs of abuse.
- Transport the baby to the hospital.
- Do not allow parents to drive themselves to the hospital.
- Provide supportive care to the parents.
- Provide accurate information.
- Be compassionate.

### SUICIDE

- Males *commit* suicide three times more often than females.
- Females *attempt* suicide three times as often as males.
- Mental illness is not necessary for a person to commit suicide.

211

## Victim's emotional state:

- Hopeless, helpless, and worthless
- Isolated
- Angry
- Depressed
- Ambivalent—wanting to live and die at the same time

## Victim's thought processes:

- Rigid
- Extremeness

## Clues to suicidal thought:

- Changes in personality, attitudes
- Depression
- Difficulty in concentrating
- Social isolation
- Decline in school or job performance
- Personal neglect
- Preparing affairs for death
- Subtle or obvious suicidal threats
- Lack of concern for oneself

## Special cautions:

- Take all suicide threats seriously.
- Suicide has a powerful negative impact on the crisis worker.
- There is often a homicidal component to suicides.

## Interventions:

- If possible, get individual to a private area.
- Tell person you want to help.
- LISTEN CAREFULLY (this is the best helping technique available).

- Validate or "okay" the person's feelings.
- Only one rescuer does the talking.
- Offer food or beverage to the individual.
- Talk directly about the suicide. Do not "beat around the bush."
- If individual questions your sincerity and your desire to help, just reaffirm that you are there to help.
- Emphasize the positive things which might help a person to lean toward life.
- Focus on the main problem, or take the problems one at a time.
- Offer alternatives.
- Do not lie or promise what you cannot give.
- Try to get individual's agreement on a specific, immediate plan of action. (For example, to talk for five to ten minutes, then to go with you to the hospital emergency room where people are willing to help.)
- Do not argue, moralize, or try to make the person feel guilty.
- Do not take unnecessary risks.
- Should a suicide attempt become a completed act while crisis workers are attempting to intervene, they should be careful not to blame themselves. Nothing they could have done would have changed the outcome if the suicidal person had made a decision to destroy himself.
- Use family intervention techniques should a suicide be completed prior to the arrival of emergency service personnel.

## VIOLENCE

- Violence is defensive. The person is attempting to maintain some form of control. The only way he may know how to maintain control is by intimidating those around him.
- Violence on the part of the crisis worker will usually only generate more violence from the victim.
- Violence is time limited. If you can delay long enough, it will subside.

213

- The best predictor of potential violence is a history of previous violence.
- Alcohol and other drugs increase the threat of violence.

## Interventions:

- Separate combatants as best as you can. The preferred method is to talk the combatants down but using force only when necessary.
- Take your time.
- Do not attempt to disarm a violent person unless you have been specially trained and have adequate help.
- Delaying frequently makes violence less likely.
- Restore as much order and control of the situation as you possibly can.
- Listen carefully to the potentially violent person.
- Try to fulfill reasonable requests to establish some rapport.
- Only one person does the negotiating.
- Do not allow interruptions.
- Offer alternatives to the potentially violent person.
- Do not touch the person until things calm down.
- Do not show weapons. They can make someone panic.
- Take all precautions to protect yourself.

# INDEX

217